INTERDEPENDENT MAGIC

INTERDEPENDENT MAGIC
DISABILITY PERFORMANCE IN CANADA

EDITED BY JESSICA WATKIN

PLAYWRIGHTS CANADA PRESS
TORONTO

Interdependent Magic: Disability Performance in Canada © Copyright 2022 by Jessica Watkin
All contributions herein are copyright © 2022 by their respective authors.
An excerpt from *Access Me* was previously published in *Canadian Theatre Review* 187, summer 2021, © University of Toronto Press.
First edition: March 2022
Printed and bound in Canada by Rapido Books, Montreal

Jacket art by Wy Joung Kou
Photos of the *Access Me* performers on page 69 © Copyright Dahlia Katz

Playwrights Canada Press
202-269 Richmond St. W., Toronto, ON M5V 1X1
416.703.0013 | info@playwrightscanada.com | www.playwrightscanada.com

No part of this book may be reproduced, downloaded, or used in any form or by any means without the prior written permission of the publisher, except for excerpts in a review or by a licence from Access Copyright, www.accesscopyright.ca.

For professional or amateur production rights, please contact Playwrights Canada Press.

LIBRARY AND ARCHIVES CANADA CATALOGUING IN PUBLICATION

Title: Interdependent magic : disability performance in Canada / edited by Jessica Watkin.
Names: Watkin, Jessica, editor.
Identifiers: Canadiana (print) 20210303026 | Canadiana (ebook) 20210303158
 | ISBN 9780369102867 (softcover) | ISBN 9780369102874 (PDF)
 | ISBN 9780369102881 (HTML)
Subjects: LCSH: People with disabilities—Drama. | LCSH: Canadian drama
 —21st century. | CSH: Canadian drama (English)—21st century
Classification: LCC PS8309.D57 I58 2021 | DDC C812.008/09207—dc23

Playwrights Canada Press operates on land which is the ancestral home of the Anishinaabe Nations (Ojibwe / Chippewa, Odawa, Potawatomi, Algonquin, Saulteaux, Nipissing, and Mississauga), the Wendat, and the members of the Haudenosaunee Confederacy (Mohawk, Oneida, Onondaga, Cayuga, Seneca, and Tuscarora), as well as Metis and Inuit peoples. It always was and always will be Indigenous land.

We acknowledge the financial support of the Canada Council for the Arts, the Ontario Arts Council (OAC), Ontario Creates, and the Government of Canada for our publishing activities.

TABLE OF CONTENTS

Finding *Interdependent Magic*: Introducing the Anthology
by Jessica Watkin
ix

Answering A Few Introductory Questions About Disability . . .
by Jessica Watkin
xv

Smudge
by Alex Bulmer
INTRODUCTION BY JESSICA WATKIN
1

Access Me
by the Boys in Chairs Collective (Andrew Gurza, Ken Harrower, Frank Hull, Debbie Patterson, Brian Postalian, and Jonathan Seinen)
INTRODUCTION BY JESSICA WATKIN
61

Neurodivergence and Interdependent Practice:
A Conversation with Niall McNeil
by Becky Gold
117

Antarctica
by Syrus Marcus Ware
INTRODUCTION BY YOUSEF KADOURA
129

Deafy
by Chris Dodd
INTRODUCTION BY DR. JENELLE ROUSE
157

About the Contributors
197

FINDING *INTERDEPENDENT MAGIC*: INTRODUCING THE ANTHOLOGY

Interdependency is both "you and I" and "we." It is solidarity, in the best sense of the word. It is inscribing community on our skin over and over and over again. It is truly moving together in an oppressive world towards liberation and refusing to let the personal be a scapegoat for the political. It is knowing that one organization, one student or community group is not a movement. It is working in coalition and collaboration.

Because the truth is: we need each other. *We need each other.* And every time we turn away from each other, we turn away from ourselves. We know this. Let us not go around, but instead, courageously through.

—Mia Mingus, *Interdependency
(excerpts from several talks)* 2020[1]

I remember
As I walk the tight rope—
this spider web—
of interdependence
As I glide gracefully from moon to moon
In my orbit
Checking in and supporting
Celebrating the joy
And holding space for pain,

---

[1] https://leavingevidence.wordpress.com/2010/01/22/interdependency-exerpts-from-several-talks/.

even though
this moon rock has never known that moon rock
The energy moves with me
And unknown gifts from strangers
Like bees pollinating from residue of other flowers
My interdependent web is pollinated by one another.

What I learn here
I carry there

And am fuelled to share more
Allow myself to open more
Ask for more
Rely on the web more
Encouraged by the vulnerability of the moons I help
The ease they share
The strength we build as I move to hold up this moon as that moon holds me up.
I smile towards the sun while the debris is in my eyes
But the rotations know the way to deliver me.

I trust in this web.
radical reciprocity, offering, and remembering.
—*Jessica Watkin* on interdependence during a pandemic, June 2020

While writing this I cannot see the words I am typing. I can see something is there, but the words are indecipherable to me. For the past decade I've experienced the world through melted detail, not able to see the faces of my loved ones, the places I loved as I grew up, or my own face in the mirror. Being Blind requires an embodied sense of space, attention, and energy. Every step I take contributes to a map of the world inside my head, it takes a lot of trust that the earth under my feet will be there when I step down. Imagine a world where every moment is informed by your memory, awareness, and energy for not only your productivity but, more importantly, your safety. The hardest part of losing my vision at eighteen was learning at light speed the necessity to trust and rely on others. I had been a high-achieving, independent teenager, and asking for help was difficult. But it became a core part of who I am to embrace what I now know as *interdependence*.

As an introvert I require substantial amounts of time on my own to recharge my nervous system, but that does not mean that I am beyond asking for support, in big and small areas of my life, because having support from others is beautiful. Demonstrating care through action, through holding space, through showing up for one another is beautiful. I've learned about interdependence from the Crip and Disability communities I am part of, but also from those around the world, and from the dreamed-up worlds that those folks have created.

Each artist in this collection touches interdependence in different ways. From dramaturgical methods that are either embodied or durational, to co-creations and multilingual pieces, to subverting expectations of "ability" and representation.

Although there's an introduction for each piece, I thought I'd introduce the artists as my friends here for you.

Alex Bulmer is a Blind theatre artist who has written plays, radio pieces, and non-visual performances, as well as curated Disability events in Canada and England. When I met Alex we made so many Blind jokes together, and us Blinkies continue to do so to this day. Niall McNeil is a Neurodivergent theatre creator and published artist. Niall always has a joke to tell me and is a warm presence in any and every room. I met Chris Dodd at the Republic of Inclusion in 2017 and was touched by his calm and inviting demeanor. Chris is a playwright and Deaf arts organizer from Edmonton, with his Deaf theatre festival *Sound Off* holding space for Deaf performances every year. The Boys in Chairs Collective consists of many folks, and the team has been working on the piece *Access Me* in different forms for a while now in Toronto. My favourite thing about this team is that it always feels like a bit of a party when we gather—lots of hugs and jokes and it is all very kind-hearted and fun. Finally, Syrus Marcus Ware is a power legend and leader. He is a visual artist, performance creator, scholar, activist, and all around kind human. My most honoured privilege with Syrus is that he always tells me who he is because he knows I cannot recognize him, and he always asks for a hug (when he can, pre-COVID).

Each contributor to this book, including the wonderful folks who wrote introductions for the pieces that they can introduce much better than I can (Yousef Kadoura, Jenelle Rouse, and Becky Gold, who not only wrote a beautifully careful introduction but also interviewed Niall for his contribution to this book), as well as my transcribing powerhouse Margeaux Feldman and the incredible cover artist Wy Joung Kou, understands the soft edges of Disability, Disability communities, and Disability art, and I am honoured to be among such a beautiful constellation of suns and stars. Within most Disability arts communities there is a quality, a texture, close to intimacy but more exciting, when we realize that we can be soft together. That feeling, for me, is a kind of interdependent magic.

What you find in this collection is not *just* scripts. Sometimes when Disabled folks create a piece, a performance, a world, I have trouble as a Disability dramaturge to refer to the text as a script. There are manifestations of performance texts here, four to be exact, and each was crafted and offered by the Disabled creators themselves. The other piece is an interview, based on intimate knowledge of creation processes, and is here to offer context and observations from the *doing*. The other piece that I'd like to highlight here is a brief primer I've included on all things Disability in a Canadian context. It is integral to me that this entire book is grounded in Disability Justice and Disability pride, and is Disability-crafted. That section is important to read prior to reading any piece of this book because although the artists and pieces in this book are brilliant, beautiful, magic humans, it isn't because of how they deal with their Disabilities (overcoming narratives). They are brilliant, beautiful, magic humans because of what they offer to the world, and it is a privilege to learn from them.

WHO IS THIS BOOK FOR?

This book is for theatre and performance lovers interested in innovative work that is Canada/Turtle Island–centred and by Disabled artists. I imagine this book in classrooms, being studied by students with fresh brains and courage. I imagine this book on the bookshelves of scholars and theatre creators, tokens of perspectives that may be completely different from their own. I imagine this book playing from headphones, being felt by hands, being translated into other accessible languages.

I offer this book as an anchor for all, for anyone, who needs a place to float on or a space to feel their own magic. It takes bravery to know that you need something outside of yourself to feel supported and to get you through. I've been there, and that is the core priority of interdependence: I, Jessica Watkin, have curated and compiled this book over many months, carefully dreaming of a day when it can fuel others for the needs that I cannot even imagine. Take what you need, and leave what others could use, too.

This book is for the Disabled artists who feel alone, who feel isolated, who feel exhausted from having to advocate for themselves on their chosen paths. This book is a small token of magic for you, dear Crip artists, to know that there is future, there is success, there are people who are like you and they want to share their magic with you. There is a community waiting for you who will warmly welcome you into the realm of Crip magic, of creative (co-) creation, and of dreaming up radically equitable, diverse, and Disability-centred futures.

Thank you for trying; thank you for existing; and thank you for being you.

Finally, this book is a celebration for all of the Disabled artists in Canada, our elders young and old, our fierce advocates and new recruits, our allies, our hearts, and our courageous and strong body-minds. This book celebrates *us* and the doing, dreaming, making, performing, manifesting, loving, and caring that comes with creating Disability art.

May this collection of words and magic bring you peace.

May this book be an anchor in trying times.

May these pages and these artists offer you space to feel joy, grief, pain, rage, excitement, and everything you need.

May this collection offer you a ramble through the worlds of fiercely talented Disabled artists, their hard work to be where they are, and their magic.

May you feel invited to this soft space of strength.

ANSWERING A FEW INTRODUCTORY QUESTIONS ABOUT DISABILITY . . .

Disclaimer: Whatever I offer here will be incomplete, but that is a core tenant of being Disabled—constantly in flux, constantly trying to keep up and recalibrate based on our surroundings, and constantly missing things. Take this loose definition with a grain of salt and as a starting point. At the end of this section, I have a Recommended Reading and Resources list to further expand on these topics.

WHAT DOES "DISABILITY" MEAN?

Disability is an experience of the world, society, and body that is unique to each individual but can be considered as experiencing barriers in society due to the ways in which society is incapable of accommodating for the broad kinds of people, minds, and bodies within it. These people, minds, and bodies function outside of what is considered "mainstream" or "normal."

Disability can be a product of birth; acquired from illness or disease later than birth; or acquired from geological, social, political, cultural, or warfare implications later than birth. (At times Disability as a product of violence or warfare is referred to as Debility via Jasbir Puar.[1]) Being Disabled does not mean someone is lacking or gaining anything but is a way in which people experience the world. Disability, or Disabled, can be an identity or state of experience. It can be painful, or prideful. Disability is more complicated and beautiful than just *not being able*.

---

1 Puar, Jasbir. *The Right to Maim: Debility, Capacity, Disability*. Duke UP, 2017.

WHY IS DISABILITY SOMETIMES CAPITALIZED, AND SOMETIMES NOT?

When Disability has the capital D it is referring to the political identity and community of Disability. For example, I, Jessica Watkin, identify as Blind and Disabled, with intentional capitalizations, because those are my political and personal identities and communities that I associate myself with. Similar to when the D in "Deaf" is capitalized compared to the lower case "deaf," the capitalization connotes an identity and community association. This is a choice made by each person, and not a universal "rule."

WHY DO YOU USE DISABILITY INSTEAD OF DIFFERENTLY ABLED, HANDICAPPED, ETC.?

The language we use in the Disability communities is intentional and subjective, meaning that language shifts person to person. I will elaborate on this more below, but for the matter of Disabled vs. Differently Abled etc., the term Disability is used to identify a community internationally and politically, and is the clearest term for what the greater majority understands as Disabled. In my experience, people who use "Differently Abled" and its counterparts are looking for a "polite" or "politically correct" way to acknowledge a Disabled person's difference without using what they consider to be "offensive language." As a Disabled person, let me assure you that any language I did not consent to is offensive. So, first rule of language is that you *ask Disabled people how they would like to be referred to.*

The second part of this debate is that Disability refers to communities and political movements that I as a Disabled person want to be associated with, while also centring the Disabled person in the title. When someone uses "Differently Abled" they center the Able-body, the "normal," as the true identity of the person; it centres the difference as opposed to the person. My second rule of language is to *centre the Disabled person.* At this point, in Canada, we use Disability.

WHAT LANGUAGE SHOULD I USE WHEN COMMUNICATING WITH DISABLED PEOPLE?

I've begun going through language rules above, but I will recap. Off the top, *always ask a Disabled person how they would like to be referred to and how they identify*. Similar to asking for someone's pronunciation of their name and their pronouns, we need to normalize asking Disabled people how they would like to be referred to within the context of Disability communities. Second, we must *centre Disability when we talk about Disability*. To unpack this guideline further I will say that this refers to language; for example, by saying *non-disabled* instead of *able-bodied* when referring to someone without Disability, see how that language centres Disability versus ability?

Here's some context on a few major terms under the umbrella of Disability that are sometimes misunderstood:

Mad: This is possible language for people who experience mental illness as their Disability.

Crip: A reclamation of the negative term *cripple*, Crip can be a verb or a noun. Noun: an identity that aligns a Disabled person with the politics of Disability, Disability Rights/Justice. Verb: *to crip* is to disrupt or intervene in a non-normal, Disability-centred way.

Disability-identified: This phrase is common when considering Disability Arts and the integration of Disability/Disabled folks with non-disabled folks. When considering, for example, a team of theatre creators and some of them are Disabled and others are not, Disabled folks on the team may use the term Disability-identified to differentiate between those in the group, similar to the phrase *with lived experience of Disability*. These are just phrases that Disabled folks may prefer as their identifiers beyond just simply identifying as Disabled.

Person-First Language: There is a lot to unpack with person-first language. What this refers to is when usually government policy refers to Disabled people as *people with Disabilities*, or *person with a Disability*. Similar to the debate between Disabled and Differently Abled, the person-first language is meant to restore dignity to Disabled people by reminding them and everyone else that they are in fact a person first, and then Disabled. This turn in language hopes to center the person's identity as a person before Disability, normally because Disability is seen as a negative thing to non-disabled people.

After following my rule of language (*ask the Disabled person which they prefer: person or Disability-first language*), what we must consider here is that Disability is not seen as a negative thing for large political Disability communities. Some Disabled people are proud of their Disability (Disability Pride is a huge political movement in North America), and so removing their preferred identifier of Disabled from their identity is not restoring dignity to them, but robbing them of the agency to be proud of their Disability and Disability identities.

Chemical Sensitivity: There may be other ways to refer to this, but it is becoming more commonly referenced in public buildings in Canada. Chemical sensitivity is when chemicals that are present in commonly used products cause irritation, illness, or emergency reactions for some people. Laundry detergents, deodorants, dish/hand soaps are all only a snapshot of some of the common items that include harmful chemicals.

Neurodivergent/Neurotypical: Neurodivergent refers to anyone who experiences the world in non-normative ways when it comes to their brains: processing, communicating, etc. You may know this better as an intellectual Disability, cognitive Disability, or from the UK, Learning Disability. (This is different than a learning Disability in Canada, which may refer to someone who is dyslexic, though this does not mean that folks who are dyslexic cannot also be neurodivergent or Disabled, but that the umbrella term does not include many other kinds of neurodivergent experiences.) Neurotypical folks are the non-disabled equivalent in this context. It refers to people whose experience is not considered divergent, but are typical. This language and these terms aren't perfect, but they are seeds that we plant to explore new ways of understanding these identities.

WHAT IS "INSPIRATION PORN"?

It is important for me to expand on what this term means as a way to contextualize this book. Inspiration porn refers to society considering a Disabled person inspirational because they exist with a Disability. This idea drips with pity, and that is not how Disabled people want to be framed in media articles, in social media messages, with family, or by strangers on the street. As a Disabled person who is an artist-scholar, I experience inspiration porn when people tell me that it's amazing that I am pursuing a graduate degree (or pursuing my undergraduate degree or, when I first lost my vision, that I was able to get out of bed in the morning).

What inspiration porn—or considering Disabled people amazing just because they live every day with a Disability—does is celebrate the lives of Disabled people and their work not for the merit of their work, but for their Disability. Inspiration porn comes from the non-disabled community.

WHAT IS DISABILITY JUSTICE?

Disability Justice is an intersectional movement and framework led by Black Indigenous People of Colour and Disability communities. It's meant to welcome and co-create ways to find justice for Disabled people, and the world we inhabit. This is a loose definition, because Disability Justice is constantly changing, subjective, and fluid. The term was coined by Sins Invalid, the Crip BIPOC gender-nonconforming performance organization, who use the following ten principles to find guidance within the objectives of the framework:

Intersectionality
Leadership from those most impacted
Anti-capitalist politics
Cross-movement solidarity
Recognizing wholeness
Sustainability
Cross-Disability solidarity

Interdependence
Collective Access
Collective Liberation

For more information, check out the Disability Justice Primer on the Sins Invalid website, which has a seven-dollar digital version for sale to support the organization, and get more context on these principles.

WHAT IS THE DIFFERENCE BETWEEN DISABILITY ARTS AND ACCESSIBILITY ARTS?

Disability Arts: Art, theatre, and performance that is created by (and possibly for) Disabled artists. This could be an integrated team of Disabled and non-disabled artists, but overall Disability Art refers to the Disability-centred, created pieces.

Accessibility Arts: Pieces of art that incorporate accessibility measures, but do not necessarily contain Disability content. Access measures may include (but are not limited to): Relaxed Performance, Audio Description, American Sign Language (ASL).

This differentiation is important because not all Accessibility Art is Disability-centred, and not all Disability Art is accessible (for all), but some may be! It is important to separate the two because if a theatre has ASL, that does not mean it is a part of what we in Canada refer to as Disability Arts, but it does advocate for the inclusion of Disabled and Deaf people through its Access measures.

RESOURCES FOR FURTHER UNDERSTANDING

DIGITAL ACCESS

Sins Invalid. *Skin, Tooth, and Bone: The Basis of Movement is Our People, a Disability Justice Primer* (https://www.sinsinvalid.org/disability-justice-primer).

Mingus, Mia. *Leaving Evidence* (www.leavingevidence.wordpress.com).

Search "#DisabilityTwitter" on Twitter

BOOKS

Hamraie, Aimi. *Building Access: Universal Design and the Politics of Disability*. U of Minnesota P, 2017.

Johnston, Kirsty. *Stage Turns: Canadian Disability Theatre*. McGill-Queen's UP, 2012.

Kafer, Alison. *Feminist, Queer, Crip*. Indiana UP, 2013.

Lakshmi Piepzna-Samarasinha, Leah. *Care Work: Dreaming Disability Justice*. Arsenal Pulp, 2018.

Wong, Alice. *Disability Visibility: First-Person Stories from the Twenty-First Century*. Vintage, 2020.

JOURNAL ARTICLES

Frazee, Catherine. "Disability in Dangerous Times." *Journal on Developmental Disabilities* 15, no. 3 (2003): 118–24. https://oadd.org/wp-content/uploads/2009/01/Frazee_15-3.pdf.

Lewis, Victoria Ann. "The Dramaturgy of Disability." *Michigan Quarterly Review* 15, no. 3 (Summer 1998): 525–39. http://hdl.handle.net/2027/spo.act2080.0037.318.

**SMUDGE
BY ALEX BULMER**

I dedicate this publication of *Smudge* to my dear missed friends Liz Dixon, Judith Snow, and Jeff Healey, three powerful disabled artists who impacted Canadian culture and remain a blessing in memory for me every day.

ACKNOWLEDGEMENTS

I'd like to thank Tristan Whiston, Kate Lynch, Lesley Lester, Sarah Garton Stanley, Diane Flacks, and Alisa Palmer for their generous contribution to this work.

INTRODUCTION
BY JESSICA WATKIN

As her Blindness began to shift and shape the ways in which she could engage with the world, Alex Bulmer's overwhelming struggle with navigating the world began. She hired Eryn Dace Trudell from Damn Straight Studios, a good friend who was also a talented choreographer, to assist with creating what Alex now refers to as "monographs" that would eventually transform into her first play *Smudge*. Alex tells me about this time:

> "[We] met once a week over a summer for two months, eight sessions together in her studios [. . . They were] two-hour sessions, and I would go in and might've written one or two words or a sentence, an idea, or a feeling. Whatever it was, it was nothing really written in any kind of developed way, based on feeling ([i.e.] "Scared; today I just can't stop imagining myself touching the world.") . . . She would put me through contact improvisations; sometimes she'd set me free, sometimes I'd be with her. I had enough partial sight so I could run freely, knowing it was a big studio . . . if I was in any danger she would shout out . . . And then we would stop after a little while, often it was because I'd say I want to write now, or it'd be because we'd been moving for fifteen minutes—time for a break; it would be when I felt [. . .] words were coming up out of my body, out of the experience; I would sit down and write, and I think I usually would use a pen and paper or I would dictate to Eryn and she would write—I never relied on technology. We did that for eight weeks, and by the end of it I had pages of writing that was then dictated back to me . . . I was way too stuck,

4 | INTERDEPENDENT MAGIC

I couldn't find the words anymore; and I knew it lived in my body and I knew that's where the most authenticity and truth would come from, and it did."

Since our discussion, Alex has shared some monographs with me. From this emerging practice that relies on other people to make the magic happen (ah, the ways in which interdependence flows) I've learned about both creating performances durationally, a common theme in Disability art, and the myriad of ways that ideas manifest in and outside of ourselves.

Here's a taste of the monographs that were the seed for *Smudge*:

VOICES

The evening passes—under a skyline of voices. I am sitting on a patio with several friends around me in the dark. No one is visible. These are familiar voices, but I need to paint them in my mind with past images. Everyone can be pictured beautiful, because they are clear and close to my skin. The imagination connects us as one. We become intimately attached.

HELD

Am I losing my sight or entering darkness?
I do not know what sight is.
Darkness is the step after the cliff edge.
For today I stand completely still.
Held by fear.

The first time I read this play was at the National Arts Centre's Republic of Inclusion and the Study, which occurred in June 2017. I had met Alex earlier in the winter and, after spending a few days together, she asked if I would read the character Freddie for her presentation day. She sent me the script and excerpts, and I was worried about reading into a mic in front of these incredible nationally acclaimed artists. I have a hard time reading in general; normally my iPad is resting on my chest and the words are super large and close to my face. How was I supposed to do this while also speaking into a desk mic? But I read the piece, and I needed to read it out loud for my peers at the Study, because the final scene ruined me. In a good way.

I remember the morning of Alex's presentation day we were in her hotel room and she was expressing to me how she wasn't sure if the last scene should be included in the presentation. I paused for a moment and replied, "Really? Because I can't get through it without crying." She asked me to do a full read for her, and during that last moment, when I just couldn't get through expressing my grief and loss over a shared losing of our sight (the "our" here is Alex and me, since I too lost my eyesight near my twenties, when Alex also lost her sight). The room went quiet, and all Alex said was, "Well, that's settled then. You have to read it." And I did, and I think folks at the Study started to see me differently (pun very much intended).

Look, I'm not a performer anymore. I like to create and tell stories, but lately I've been much more into advocacy, dramaturgy, and research. But I know how to read, and especially when a piece settles into your psyche in a way that it cannot crawl its way out. It felt as though Freddie hadn't just crawled into me, but was me.

Mia Mingus talks about access intimacy being that visceral, unspoken, and inarticulable feeling when you meet someone, disabled or not, who just *gets* you. You don't need to explain to them why you need access in a certain way, or why something bothers you, or the hardships you go through—they just already know. This was the first true time I'd felt that in an art space, that not only had Alex captured this feeling I thought I was isolated in for so long (at that point it had nearly been a ten-year journey for me through my eye surgeries and Blindness), but she'd also set the tone for how access intimacy works as a fluid state within the Disability Arts communities in Canada.

I was reading the words about loss of my sight as a person who had acquired Disability later in life, like Alex had and like Freddie does in *Smudge*, but there were people at the Study and other creators in this book who have lived with their Disabilities since birth. These are two different and valid experiences of Disability, but what comes with both is the intimate understanding and lived experience of oppression and barriers in Canada.

Smudge explores relationships that a Disabled queer woman navigates while understanding a life without sight, or as us Blind folks sometimes say: a life with Blindness. Freddie hears her diagnosis; experiences her personal romantic relationship changing to reflect a different way of caring for one another; and ultimately experiences a shift in her, represented by the figure of an "Entity" whose physical presence hovers close by, a comfort and a reflection. The fragmented scenes remind me of sifting through memories, trying to reconcile understandings of the world, a new world. As a Blind person this piece makes me feel *seen*. My experiences of loss in the world are captured and held in this piece, and what feels inarticulable to me is articulated in the text and texture of *Smudge*.

So regularly narratives about Disability and gaining a Disability centres an overcoming of obstacles, the obstacles being disruptions in what is widely considered as "normal." What we can learn from Disabled people, artists, and art is that by deviating from the norm and from experiencing the world "normally," we learn more about what it means to be human. Also, so regularly are narratives about Disabled people created by non-disabled people, and this book holds space for Disabled people telling their own stories, a perspective that is full of complexity, nuance, humour, and grief. *Smudge* asks readers to consider their relationship to sight, vision, and Blindness and the ways in which we experience the world. If the Entity is a reflecting tool for Freddie, then *Smudge* is a reflecting tool for its readers: not on Disability or ableism, but to reflect on our ways of engaging with each other.

Smudge was first produced by Nightwood Theatre in association with S.N.I.F.F. Inc. at the Tarragon Back Space, Toronto, in November 2000, with the following cast and creative team:

Freddie: Diane Flacks
Katherine / Others: Kate Lynch
The Entity / Others: Sherry Lee Hunter

Director: Alisa Palmer
Set and Costume Design: Carolyn M. Smith
Lighting Design: Andrea Lundy
Sound Design: John Gzowski and Debashis Sinha
Stage Manager: Fiona Jones

Smudge was nominated for a Chalmers Award for Best New Play, and a Dora Mavor Moore Award for Best Play, Best Production, and Best Lighting Design. *Smudge* was also produced in the UK by In Tandem TC and earned a Time Out Magazine Critics Choice Award.

CHARACTERS

Freddie: A young woman who is losing her sight

Katherine: Her girlfriend

The Entity: An inextricable presence, a facet of Freddie's mind and soul.

Many Others who come and go in Freddie's darkening world

SET

The stage is bare, except for a single chair with a white cane resting on it. A scrim divides upstage from downstage, and beyond that is a mirrored wall. The reflection of the chair is seen through the murky scrim in the upstage mirror. Throughout the play, Freddie appears in front of the scrim. The Entity begins behind the scrim, appearing as a shadow, a ghost, a memory of sight, a fantasy of vision. As the play progresses, the Entity moves closer and closer to Freddie, finally entering Freddie's world.

SCENE ONE: IMAGINATION

FREDDIE, with her cane and glasses, stands alone on stage.

During the course of the opening monologue, a silent screen star becomes visible upstage of the scrim.

FREDDIE: I imagine myself a wild and crazy silent screen star who has had an unfortunate accident and is suddenly left blind. She insists upon continuing with her career despite everyone's disapproval. She demands tighter shots and less movement on set. She never moans, grieves, or complains. A cutting moment occurs during a break. A young girl innocently asks Estelle—we'll call her Estelle—"Estelle, what's it like to be blind?" Estelle turns and says quite matter-of-factly:

FREDDIE & THE ENTITY: "Boring. Dead, outright boring."

THE ENTITY: My life as a silent screen star is based on the unexpected. Shocks, tricks, escape. I give people what they don't expect, can't predict, and walk away with a tremendous grin. But this, my dear, this is the ultimate humdrum, anti-drama. This unfortunate addition to me is my disaster. Boring, boring, and I refuse to be boring."

The word "Smudge" appears from the darkness as the silent screen star's light fades. The word slowly disappears.

10 | **INTERDEPENDENT MAGIC**

SCENE TWO: HOSPITAL

#1

> A hospital TECHNICIAN stands beside FREDDIE.

FREDDIE: E M P

TECHNICIAN: Anything? Anything else?

FREDDIE: A fuzzy worm?

> FREDDIE *looks at the* TECHNICIAN, *puzzled.*

> *Blackout.*

#2

TECHNICIAN: Okay, "Fingers or Fist." Fingers or fist?

> *The* TECHNICIAN *moves her hand to the left, and to the right, top and bottom alternating between fingers and fist at each position.*

FREDDIE: Fist. Fingers. Fingers. Fist. Fingers.

> *The* TECHNICIAN *moves her hand toward the centre.*

Fist. Fisht—fishters—sishticks—shingers—scissors!

TECHNICIAN: What?

FREDDIE: Rock, paper, scissors.

> FREDDIE *demonstrates with her hand.*

Ready? One, two, three.

They play.

TECHNICIAN: Dynamite! I win!

Blackout.

#3

TECHNICIAN: Follow my finger.

The TECHNICIAN *traces her finger from right to left in front of* FREDDIE's *face.*

FREDDIE *is able to follow to the centre, and then stops.*

The TECHNICIAN *continues with her finger to the left.*

FREDDIE *is frozen, looking straight ahead. Her eyes jump to the far left, catching a glimpse of the finger tracing left of her face.*

The TECHNICIAN's *hand moves right, and to the centre, and up.*

FREDDIE *follows and, assuming the hand will go straight to the right, she looks that way. Realizing it's not there,* FREDDIE *searches with her peripheral vision to find the* TECHNICIAN's *hand.*

When she does:

Are you following my fingers or are you guessing?

FREDDIE: I'm not sure there's a difference.

12 | INTERDEPENDENT MAGIC

The TECHNICIAN *touches* FREDDIE's *nose.* FREDDIE *doesn't see it—she's startled.*

Blackout.

#4

TECHNICIAN: Look at this picture. What do you see?

FREDDIE: A bunch of dots.

TECHNICIAN: In the dots what do you see?

FREDDIE: Um, in the dots—in the dots?

TECHNICIAN: There's a picture in the dots. You can't see it?

FREDDIE: Wait, in the dots! Two people having sex. Three people having sex? Oh! A star!

TECHNICIAN: I suspect that you're guessing. Look right into the dots. Would you say it looks like a dolphin?

FREDDIE: No.

TECHNICIAN: No? Are you sure?

FREDDIE: No, I do not see a dolphin.

TECHNICIAN: You don't see a dolphin?

FREDDIE: Yes, that is what I said.

TECHNICIAN: No dolphin.

FREDDIE: That is what I've always said! No dolphin!

Enter FREDDIE's *mind's eye. The* TECHNICIAN *is suddenly transformed into an* SS *Gestapo officer.*

TECHNICIAN: And yet we have you on record as seeing a dolphin several times. In fact, I believe you saw a dolphin yesterday in the Soviet embassy!

FREDDIE: That is a lie!

TECHNICIAN: Is it? Look at the next picture!

FREDDIE: No! No! No!

TECHNICIAN: Do you by any chance see the code number 786 X R P?

FREDDIE: No! You will never get away with this! I'll never tell you anything. No matter what you do to me. You will never break me! I'll tell nothing! I see nothing!

A return to reality.

The TECHNICIAN *watches* FREDDIE *with mild concern.*

Nothing!

TECHNICIAN: I think we'll stop here.

FREDDIE: I thought you said we were going to do a couple more.

TECHNICIAN: We did. You didn't see them. We'll rest your eyes now.

The TECHNICIAN *places a blindfold over* FREDDIE's *eyes and exits.*

SCENE THREE: DOCTOR

DR. DUVALL *enters carrying a clipboard.*

DR. DUVALL: Hello, Freddie. I'm Dr. Duvall. This must be very difficult for you.

FREDDIE: I'm all right. Can you tell me some results?

DR. DUVALL: The technicians say you're quite a pleasure to work with.

FREDDIE: Yeah. I like them too. So what did you find?

DR. DUVALL: Just wait one moment.

DR. DUVALL *writes notes on her file.*

FREDDIE: I know I bombed the colour test.

DR. DUVALL *is still writing.*

DR. DUVALL: Just wait one moment.

FREDDIE: And the field test was a big bust.

DR. DUVALL: Just a moment.

DR. DUVALL *finishes writing.*

FREDDIE: The red dye stuff made me barf.

DR. DUVALL: It did, yes. That's a reaction that can happen.

FREDDIE: I barfed three times.

DR. DUVALL: You're probably allergic to the red fluorescence. It can make some patients' heart race and it can be a cause of nausea. I'm sorry you had to go through that. We won't need to do that test again for a few years.

FREDDIE: So, I'm coming back then?

DR. DUVALL: Yes. What I'm seeing appears to be an atypical dystrophy of the rods and cones, pigmenting of the cells. It looks like spider webs in the back of the eye.

FREDDIE: Oh. What do yours look like?

DR. DUVALL: In a healthy eye, the cells regenerate and the back of the eye is clear. Yours are scarred.

FREDDIE: So, how bad does it get, the scars?

DR. DUVALL: As far as we know the scarring progresses and eventually leaves the eye with only light and shadow perception. It is a genetic blindness. In your case you have what is called recessive retinitis pigmentosa inversa.

FREDDIE: Sorry, retinisis . . .

DR. DUVALL: Retinitis pigmentosa. We call it R.P. for short.

FREDDIE: We do.

DR. DUVALL: In normal retinitis pigmentosa, the loss of vision begins at the periphery and gradually moves to the centre. In your case, retinitis pigmentosa inversa, the loss of sight begins in the centre and moves toward the periphery. You can see the doughnut, but not the hole, as it were. On the other hand, that's a very good definition of an optimist, isn't it?

FREDDIE: Okay, so what are we gonna do about it?

DR. DUVALL: I can't tell you that.

FREDDIE: Do you mean, I can't tell you that because it's a doctor's secret and we're not sharing, or I can't tell you that because you don't know?

DR. DUVALL: Because we don't know. I will know more each time I see what stage the vision is at. Your condition has no cure, at present. No cure.

> *The* ENTITY, *appearing behind the scrim, raises arms to heaven, slowly lowers them to sides, and looks at* FREDDIE.

FREDDIE: This is a jolly moment. And you do this for a living?

DR. DUVALL: It's very difficult telling people that they're going to lose something so precious, so vital.

FREDDIE: Well, people must survive, otherwise there wouldn't be a CIBC.

DR. DUVALL: CNIB. Yes. We'll get you signed up. I just signed up a little baby this morning. It was very sad. I understand what it is to lose something so precious, so necessary. I spent eight months in bed as a child with polio and I learned the hard way how valuable things are. How much I thanked God I could see, since I wasn't able to do much of anything else. I couldn't go to school or play with anyone. I know how quickly things change and how painful that can be. Just the other night I came home from school, Christina's school, a parent-teacher meeting, and when I got home, the car was gone from the garage, and Barry had just suddenly left me.

> DR. DUVALL *breaks down.*

FREDDIE: Oh, I'm sorry.

DR. DUVALL: Thank you. We can take the blindfold off shortly.

(in tears) Would you like a cup of coffee?

> *She begins to rush off.*

FREDDIE: Sure. And sorry about—

DR. DUVALL: *(exiting, tears again)* Thank you.

FREDDIE: —Barry!

> *The ENTITY approaches FREDDIE, gently touches her on the shoulder.*
>
> *FREDDIE reacts to the touch.*
>
> *Then, the ENTITY removes the blindfold.*
>
> *FREDDIE reacts to the light.*

SCENE FOUR: OUTSIDE

FREDDIE: How do you know what you can't see?

> *FREDDIE looks and sees.*

Red car. Royal Bank. Old man. Blue sky.
I like to think the next few years will be just like always. I'll still see and when it comes, it comes.
Look . . . at the . . . pigeons!

> *FREDDIE waves her arms at them.*
>
> *The ENTITY mirrors the pigeon's flight behind the scrim.*

SCENE FIVE: THE DYKE CLUB

Dance music blares.

FREDDIE is alone, centre, in a tight pool of light, with a cigarette in her hand and a lighter.

She puts the cigarette in her mouth, backwards, and tries to light it.

As she vainly attempts to light her smoke, a BAR BABE crosses down to FREDDIE and turns her cigarette around.

BAR BABE: It's backwards.

The BAR BABE crosses left of FREDDIE and bends over to tie her own shoe.

A WAITRESS crosses down to FREDDIE with a beer.

WAITRESS: Coming through, coming through, here's your beer, lady.

Hands it to FREDDIE, and crosses upstage.

FREDDIE tries to drink her beer, but there is a cup over the bottle.

FREDDIE removes the cup and drinks.

Mistaking the back of the BAR BABE on her left for a table, she places the unwanted cup on the BAR BABE's back.

The BAR BABE stands, and the cup falls.

The BAR BABE bends to tie her other shoe, facing downstage.

> FREDDIE *touches her back—or table—again to make sure it's still there.*
>
> *The* BAR BABE *is annoyed by the touch, and crosses upstage of* FREDDIE.
>
> FREDDIE *tries to put her beer on the "table," but it is gone, and she bobs up and down to the music with her beer, to cover her faux pas.*
>
> *The* WAITRESS *enters again. She asks* FREDDIE *to pick up the fallen cup.*

Would you pick that up?

> FREDDIE *bends over to pick it up, but cannot see it.*
>
> *All the while, a* PATRON *noisily orders drinks from the* WAITRESS.
>
> *The* WAITRESS *is frustrated by* FREDDIE's *inability to help.*

Don't bother, I'll get it myself.

> *The* WAITRESS *crosses downstage of* FREDDIE *to retrieve the cup, barely missing stepping on her hand.*
>
> DANCER 1 *wildly flails over the top of a still crouching* FREDDIE. FREDDIE *stands up and accidentally hits* DANCER 1, *who regains her composure in time with the music.*
>
> DANCER 2 *dances up to* FREDDIE *and* DANCER 1.

DANCER 2: You are so sexy. You are so hot. Come here and give me a big kiss.

FREDDIE puckers up and moves downstage, but DANCER 2 *has grabbed* DANCER 1 *and plants a huge kiss on her. They embrace, and* DANCER 1 *carries* DANCER 2 *away.*

FREDDIE is left alone with her cigarette and beer bottle.

DANCER 3 dances up to FREDDIE, silently.

FREDDIE is lighting her smoke inadvertently in DANCER 3's face.

DANCER 3 waves the smoke away.

FREDDIE doesn't notice.

DANCER 3 coughs loudly in FREDDIE's face.

The cigarette is still not lit.

FREDDIE: Can you cover your mouth when you do that!

DANCER 3 crosses upstage of FREDDIE in disgust.

The WAITRESS crosses down to FREDDIE.

WAITRESS: Coming through, coming through. Empties, got any empties?

FREDDIE holds her bottle in the air, afraid of being bumped again.

The WAITRESS takes her beer away and crosses right.

From both left and right people start yelling:

"Freddie!" "Freddie!"

Confused as to where the voices are coming from, FREDDIE reluctantly raises her arm to wave.

SCENE SIX: LIBRARY

FREDDIE stands centre.

The LIBRARIAN is to her right with her back to FREDDIE.

A LIBRARY PATRON behind the scrim looks for a book.

FREDDIE: Hello?

LIBRARIAN: Ssssh!

FREDDIE approaches the desk.

How can I help you?

FREDDIE: Ah, yes. I'm looking for a journal.

LIBRARIAN: Yes, a journal?

FREDDIE: Yes. A journal. A medical kind of journal.

LIBRARIAN: Yes, a medical journal.

FREDDIE: Yes.

LIBRARIAN: That would be in the medical section. Just over there.

The LIBRARIAN nods her head in a direction that FREDDIE cannot see.

FREDDIE: Where?

LIBRARIAN: Just over there to the left.

FREDDIE: The left?

The LIBRARIAN turns to face FREDDIE.

LIBRARIAN: Yes, just over there to the right.

FREDDIE: To the right?

The LIBRARIAN turns back.

LIBRARIAN: To the left.

FREDDIE: To the left or right? Which is it?

LIBRARIAN: Well, it's to your left if you're standing this way, but to the right if you're facing—

FREDDIE: Right. Um, I'm looking for something specific.

LIBRARIAN: Yes?

FREDDIE: About eyes and conditions

LIBRARIAN: Eyes and conditions. Yes.

FREDDIE: For a friend of mine

LIBRARIAN: A friend, yes.

FREDDIE: She, uh, has dyslexia.

LIBRARIAN: Oh, dyslexia, that's neurology. That's just over there.

The LIBRARIAN points in the opposite direction.

FREDDIE: No, no, it's eyes. I'm sure it's eyes.

LIBRARIAN: No, no, my dear, it's neurology—

FREDDIE: It's eyes.

LIBRARIAN: Neurology.

FREDDIE: No, it's eyes. I know it's eyes because I have it.

LIBRARIAN: Oh, my dear girl. Never be ashamed of your disability. Just say, "I have dyslexia!"

FREDDIE: I have dyslexia!

LIBRARIAN: Shhhh! That's right.

FREDDIE: I have trouble reading things from left to right. So, could you take me to the medical section?

LIBRARIAN: Of course I can. Now, how would you read that? Section medical?

FREDDIE: No.

LIBRARIAN: I would be happy to get your book for you and read it to you.

FREDDIE: No, no, that's okay.

LIBRARIAN: Oh, I'd be happy to—

FREDDIE: It's okay, I'll read it.

LIBRARIAN: No, no, because how will you read it forward? Backwards?

FREDDIE: You don't have to. I'll—

LIBRARIAN: I want to, it's no trouble—

FREDDIE: No. Look, I don't even have dyslexia.

LIBRARIAN: Oh?

FREDDIE: I have R.P.

LIBRARIAN: Received Pronunciation. Linguistics, that's downstairs . . .

> The LIBRARIAN starts to direct her in another direction.

FREDDIE: No, it's retini, retinisis—

LIBRARIAN: Retinisis?

FREDDIE: Retinisis—

LIBRARIAN: Retinisiss—

FREDDIE: Resinissin—

LIBRARIAN: Resisin—

FREDDIE: Pigmenso, pigisis—

LIBRARIAN: Pigmesis—

FREDDIE: Pig, pig, pig—

> In her effort FREDDIE is suddenly, momentarily, transformed into a pig.
>
> She squeals, then stops suddenly with—

Retinitis pigmentosa!

LIBRARY PATRON: Shhhhh!

LIBRARIAN: Oh! Retinitis pigmentosa! That's in the medical section. Just over there.

The LIBRARIAN *points, but* FREDDIE *can't see where.*

SCENE SEVEN: READING

FREDDIE *holds a sheet of paper, trying to read the information she retrieved at the library.*

FREDDIE *reads only from small spots of vision available to her from the outside corner of each eye.*

Reading for FREDDIE *at this stage in her blindness means holding the page close to the outside of each eye and moving it as her vision shifts each moment. It is an elaborate, time-consuming, and fatiguing activity.*

The ENTITY, *upstage of the scrim, physicalizes and expands on* FREDDIE's *efforts.*

Both hold a piece of paper.

FREDDIE: *(slowly and with increasing difficulty)* Retinitis pigmentosa is a series of hereditary eye diseases affecting the eye. Retinitis pigmentosa is a series of heredit . . . The vision de . . . gen . . . er . . . The vision degenerates, leaving the eye with light and shadow perception. Total blindness may occur. It may affect one in thirteen thousand. Those affected complain of disjointed images, fogginess, and difficulty adjusting to changes of light.

FREDDIE *stops reading, stands, and describes what she sees.*

Foggy Jell-O.
Like looking through a straw.
Mud splattered on a windshield.

The world looks filthy.
Slash of light!
Flashing Picassos.
It's wild.
It's a picture party.
It's a mess.

SCENE EIGHT: SITTING

>   FREDDIE *enters a café.*
>
>   *People bump into her, leaving her disorientated.*
>
>   *We hear: "Excuse me" and "Hey!" from the bumpers.*

FREDDIE: "Sorry!"

>   *She sees something.*
>
>   FREDDIE *makes her way toward a chair.*
>
>   *We hear her thoughts.*
>
>   *The* ENTITY, *behind the scrim, playfully accompanies* FREDDIE's *imagination with movement.*

The light catches the edge of the chair and gleams its existence into my eyes. My hand rests on my left thigh preparing for an unknown reach. I'm expecting six inches and make contact far sooner. My fingers find the cold hard steel of a frame. Exploding out of its hardness is a soft bulge. My palm widens, my mind goes to my hand. Feels like leather. Feels like red. This is the chair. My right knee guides me toward the ninety-degree angle. My knee leads me across the frame. Reaching down, I give myself the assurance that I have found the centre. Go. Down with butt. Impact. When both hands are at equal distance from my hips, I know I have achieved optimum sitting position. My legs cross one over the other. I lean seductively forward. I smile with a twinkle, hoping to divert my audience from recognizing the efforts invested in such a simple action.

FREDDIE is smiling with self-congratulation.

FREDDIE doesn't realize that she is staring straight at another woman in the café.

KATHERINE: Hi.

FREDDIE: *(startled)* Hi. Who are you?

KATHERINE: I'm Katherine

FREDDIE beams.

SCENE NINE: CAFÉ SIGHTINGS

FREDDIE and KATHERINE sit facing each other.

FREDDIE stares straight ahead, never moving her eyes.

KATHERINE waves her fingers up to her left, then up to her right, down at centre, down left, and down right.

Each time FREDDIE nods in the affirmative.

Then KATHERINE waves her fingers at FREDDIE in the left corner of FREDDIE's vision.

FREDDIE sees this too.

KATHERINE then brings her face toward her own hand until FREDDIE can catch a glimpse of her.

FREDDIE, *seeing* KATHERINE's *face, waves back at* KATHERINE, *smiles gently, and says:*

FREDDIE: Hi.

SCENE TEN: THE MOVIES

KATHERINE *whispers a description of the movie into* FREDDIE's *ear.*

Behind them, some guy is eating popcorn.

KATHERINE: She just threw her head back and—close-up shot of her face—she groans—I guess you know that—oh, he's making a move, yup, there goes the hand.

FREDDIE: Where?

KATHERINE: Right up her shirt— Inside—

FREDDIE: Inside? Where?

KATHERINE: Inside. You know. Okay, she's quivering her lips again, there's a shot of the leftovers by the sink, he's carrying her to the sink—

FREDDIE: Is he putting her on the leftovers?

KATHERINE: No—he just propped her right in the sink-well, in front of it—her shirt's off now, she has perfect round breasts, of course.

FREDDIE: Of course.

KATHERINE: He's kissing her neck.

FREDDIE: How?

KATHERINE: It looks like a bit of tongue sliding—

FREDDIE: How?

KATHERINE: —and now he's nibbling her ear—

FREDDIE: How, nibbling?

KATHERINE: Well, it looks like lip nibbling—no, pulling maybe. And he's—oh now they're going into the bedroom—he's moving down her leg with his face—

FREDDIE: Moving where?

KATHERINE: Down to her feet and she's—you can hear that—

FREDDIE: I heard that.

KATHERINE: He's staring at her feet, oh, okay now, now he's sucking your toes—

FREDDIE: My toes? What about my toes?

KATHERINE: Her toes. He's sucking her toes.

FREDDIE: He's sucking your toes.

KATHERINE: He's sucking your toes.

FREDDIE: Ohhhh.

KATHERINE: Now, he's sliding his hands down her pants—

FREDDIE: She's bearing down waiting—holding back—

KATHERINE: He's taking his time, feeling every inch of her as he moves down—

FREDDIE: She's hot.

KATHERINE: She's on fire.

FREDDIE: She says—

SOME GUY: Will you shut up!

FREDDIE & KATHERINE: Oh, sorry.

Pause. They laugh.

FREDDIE: God, this is a really boring movie, eh?

KATHERINE: Yeah. I'm really bored.

They look at each other.

FREDDIE & KATHERINE: Let's go!

SCENE ELEVEN: THE DYKE CLUB

Dance music blares.

FREDDIE and KATHERINE slow dance at centre.

The WAITRESS enters from left with two beers, crosses centre, and hands them to KATHERINE, who hands one to FREDDIE.

FREDDIE begins to search for her money, but KATHERINE has beaten her to the punch and pays.

The WAITRESS *exits off left.*

They dance.

SCENE TWELVE: THE SECOND CUP

FREDDIE *describes what she sees.*

During the text, two figures upstage of the scrim transform from coffee-shop patrons to flamboyant flamenco dancers, flashes of FREDDIE's *fantasy.*

FREDDIE: I'm sitting at the Second Cup.

FREDDIE *leans her chin on her hand and notices—*

My fingers are sticky. I have cream cheese all over my face. I have to get a serviette. It's a big decision; it means getting up and moving across the table-cluttered room to the stuff stand. It's dire. I'm covered in goo. I go. I see the east-west parameters of this café minefield. I find my markers and place myself between them. Hey! I see the piled-up stuff. This would be the serviette centre—or someone's piley-up hairdo. I stop, I stare. I focus. Ha ha! I see something. It could be a serviette holder. I hold it. I stare at it. I stare it down like a matador. I won't be fooled. I won't reach out expecting paper wipes and make surprising contact with plastic forks. I stare with indignation. Nothing I perceive bears resemblance to anything other than the serviette holder. The white contrasting the dark shiny thing gives all my suspicions the assurance to reach out. I'm convinced. I reach out a little more to the left, now down, over, yes! Serviettes! *Fucking ace! I rule!*

FREDDIE *waves her arms in triumph and bashes a woman next to her.*

WOMAN: Oh my God, you got it all over my sweater—

FREDDIE: Oh, I'm so sorry.

SCENE THIRTEEN: THE GREAT OUTDOORS

FREDDIE on the street.

PEDESTRIANS 1 and 2 play a bevy of characters, an urban whirlwind around FREDDIE.

PEDESTRIAN 1: Excuse me—

PEDESTRIAN 2: Taxi, taxi—

PEDESTRIAN 1 speaks into a cellphone.

PEDESTRIAN 1: I want that delivered by three. Are you listening to me? Are you listening to me?

FREDDIE: What?

PEDESTRIAN 2: Hey, lady, got any spare change?

FREDDIE takes off her knapsack to look for change.

PEDESTRIAN 1: Would you like to buy some flowers?

FREDDIE turns and inadvertently bashes the flower lady in the gut with the knapsack. Flowers go everywhere.

PEDESTRIAN 2: Watch out for the doggy doo!

They all high step over it.

A DEAF WOMAN *taps* FREDDIE *on the shoulder, indicates she is Deaf, and tries to sell* FREDDIE *an* ASL *alphabet.*

FREDDIE: What?

PEDESTRIAN 1: Excuse me.

PEDESTRIAN 1 *is trying to pass by* FREDDIE *and the* DEAF WOMAN.

FREDDIE: Just a second.

The DEAF WOMAN *signs again.*

What!!

PEDESTRIAN 1: Excuse me!

FREDDIE: *(turns to* PEDESTRIAN 1*)* Just a second!!

The DEAF WOMAN *taps* FREDDIE *on the shoulder.*

(turns to PEDESTRIAN 1*)* What!!!

PEDESTRIAN 1: What are you, blind?!

PEDESTRIAN 1 *pushes past* FREDDIE, *spinning her around.*

SCENE FOURTEEN: ELEVATOR MUSIC

FREDDIE *stands in a crowded elevator.*

ELEVATOR PASSENGER 1: Press three, please.

Beat.

34 / INTERDEPENDENT MAGIC

    ELEVATOR PASSENGER 2: Press three, please.

    FREDDIE is oblivious.

    ELEVATOR PASSENGER 1: Could you press three, please?

    ELEVATOR PASSENGER 2: Press three! For chrissakes!

    PASSENGER 1 pushes past FREDDIE to push the button herself.

    ELEVATOR PASSENGER 1: Excuse me, I have to get out! This is my floor!

    Both PASSENGERS exit the elevator, shoving FREDDIE out.

    A WOMAN comes up to FREDDIE.

WOMAN: Freddie!! Freddie! Freddie, Freddie!!! Guess who. Guess! Come on, guess, guess, guess who, guess who, come on, come on, guess!!!

    FREDDIE freezes as we hear her name distort into a high-pitched confusion.

SCENE FIFTEEN: DENISE'S CANE LESSON

    FREDDIE stands with DENISE, her cane instructor.

DENISE: Using a cane requires a whole new focus for movement than you used as a sighted person. The focus is lower. You gather information with your kinesthetic sense, your ears, and your residual vision. To start, can I see your current technique with the cane?

    FREDDIE tries to walk with the cane.

Okay, so you've got no technique. Don't even bother with the ID cane. I'm thinking a forty-eight-inch Louis Hébert, with a roller tip and a golf-club grip.

FREDDIE: I'm thinking the same thing, Denise.

DENISE: Good. Okay. Starting with your grip. Hold the cane in front of you and shake hands with it. Shake hands with your cane.

SCENE SIXTEEN: OUTDOORS AGAIN

Wearing sunglasses, FREDDIE *walks down the street tapping her cane rhythmically from side to side.*

FREDDIE: Legally blind, criminally sighted. Blind, blind drunk, blind faith, blind as a bat, blindfold, Venetian blinds, Helen Keller, Stevie Wonder, John Milton, Oedipus, Three Mice, professional German Shepherds, piano tuners, piano tuners, piano tuners.

FREDDIE bumps into someone on the street.

GOTH GIRL: Watch it, crap face.

FREDDIE: Sorry, I—

GOTH GIRL: I didn't know!

FREDDIE: What?

GOTH GIRL: You don't see?

FREDDIE: A bit.

GOTH GIRL: Are you blind?

FREDDIE: Partially. Mostly.

GOTH GIRL: *(to her* FRIEND*)* Is she blind?

FRIEND OF GOTH GIRL: She just told you. She should know.

GOTH GIRL: I didn't know! Here, have some cigarettes.

FREDDIE: No, thank you.

GOTH GIRL: Here's three. I'm sorry. I didn't know. I'm not a bad person.

FREDDIE: I'm sure you're not.

GOTH GIRL: I'm sorry. You're nice.

    A man approaches FREDDIE.

MAN: Giss yer blind, eh.

FREDDIE: Partially.

MAN: I'd help the blind. Honestly, I would. Honestly.

FREDDIE: I'm sure you would.

MAN: Sorry.

    The man describes the building across the street.

Eeet's a brownish beeeelding witz layters on eet.

(as they cross the street) Green now.

    They walk.

Streetcar tracks—streetcar tracks.

    Describing the building as they approach.

Eet has white layters . . . gold treem and eeet say: Star Boooo—Star Buck. For coffee—

FREDDIE turns to elude the man.

—tea, and things like donut—

At the corner, a woman with a tight grip approaches FREDDIE *at the crossing.*

GRIPPER: Oh, I'll tell you when you can cross.

FREDDIE: That's okay, I can handle traffic.

GRIPPER: It's still red, still red, still reeeeeeeeeeeed—GREEN! Here, I'll take you.

FREDDIE: No, it's okay, I'm fine.

GRIPPER: I can't see very well, either. There's a hematoma in my left eye. My boyfriend, Jerry, hit me upside the head. Okay, about five feet from the curb, ready, two three one, STEP!

FREDDIE: Okay, I'm stopping for the streetcar now, so I'll just say bye.

GRIPPER: How did you know it was a streetcar stop?

FREDDIE: I can see sort of.

GRIPPER: Can you see colour? My boyfriend says he's colour-blind, says he can't do the laundry 'cause he'll mix it up.

FREDDIE: I think he's lying.

GRIPPER: Can you tell what I look like?

FREDDIE: Ummmm, actually, I just sense auras.

GRIPPER: What's mine?

38 | INTERDEPENDENT MAGIC

FREDDIE: Emergency red. Take care of that eye.

FREDDIE gets on the streetcar. An OLD MAN approaches.

OLDIE: *(loudly)* GOD BLESS YOU.

FREDDIE: THANK YOU. GOD BLESS YOU.

OLDIE: I DELIVERED BOXES TO THE CNIB FOR FORTY-NINE YEARS.

FREDDIE: GOODNESS.

OLDIE: WIFE WORKED THERE. TAUGHT MAKING FRIDGE MAGNETS.

FREDDIE: WELL, GOODNESS ME.

OLDIE: COULDN'T THINK OF ANYTHING WORSE THAN WHAT YOU'VE GOT.

FREDDIE: WELL, MAYBE YOU'RE NOT THINKING HARD ENOUGH.

OLDIE: EH?

FREDDIE: THERE'S DEATH.

OLDIE: EH? GOD BLESS YOU.

FREDDIE: And God bless you and thank God this is my stop.

SCENE SEVENTEEN: DINING WITH MY GIRL

FREDDIE and KATHERINE are at a restaurant.

The ENTITY appears behind the scrim, FREDDIE's private shadow.

FREDDIE: So, I'm walking here and some guy walks by and I ask him if there's a variety store nearby. I don't have my cane with me but, of course, there's a store right behind me. So the guy probably thought I was a lunkhead. So, I wander my way into the store and there's all these tough gas-station men in there and they're wanting to help me. I kept saying no, then blankly staring in hopes of any toiletry section or Kleenex. Eventually I knew I had to ask the guy behind the counter. "Excuse me, do you have Tampax?" Dead silence. "Tampax, do you carry Tampax?" "What's Tampax?" "Tampax, Tampax tampons, in a small box?" "Oh no, we don't carry that sort of thing, but, um, we do have Certs!"

She laughs.

KATHERINE: They've finally got spicy Thai bundles on the menu.

FREDDIE: What am I gonna do with a packet of Certs? I'm not sure they'll work very well.

KATHERINE: Do you want a salad? I think I'm going to have a salad tonight.

FREDDIE: Ah, yeah, I'll have the unscented breath mints with the flushable applicator, please?

KATHERINE: The goat cheese salad is $6.50 and the pear salad is $6.25.

FREDDIE: Ha ha ha.

Pause.

Well, I thought it was funny.

KATHERINE: Oh, rats, the Thai bundles are made with peanut oil. I can't have that. Oh, and they've taken my favourite bean dip off the menu.

FREDDIE: Well, that's just terrible. Does it devastate you?

KATHERINE: No, I'll find an alternative. It wouldn't be very smart if I didn't. It would be senseless not to eat just because what I wanted was no longer available.

FREDDIE: I think I'll have the Thai bundles.

KATHERINE: That's nice of you to order something that could stop my breathing.

FREDDIE: Well, your sense of humour's no breath of fresh air!

KATHERINE: I did not have my sense of humour surgically removed.

FREDDIE: Well, you're a real Thai bundle of laughs tonight.

KATHERINE: You know, strangely enough, hearing stories about you wandering around without your cane somehow doesn't strike my funny bone.

FREDDIE: Well, that wasn't the point of my story.

KATHERINE: Well, that's what I got out of it.

FREDDIE: It's a funny story about buying Tampax!

KATHERINE: Yeah, it's especially funny that you didn't have your cane. Ha! Maybe next time you go out for toilet paper, you'll get hit by a bus. That'll be hilarious!

FREDDIE: Well, you know what? I guess I'm just a big suck. Why would I want to leave my cane behind? I should love using it. It's just a big white stick. I'm sure everyone has one! Sure! Hey, why don't you go out with a nut on your head and a sign that says "I'm allergic to peanut oil"?!

KATHERINE: That is so ridiculous.

They laugh together.

FREDDIE: I just have this clear image of you with a big nut coming out of your head.

KATHERINE: Yeah, I could hang around with coconut and I'd be trail mix.

FREDDIE: Ha!

KATHERINE: Wipe your right arm, you've just got a bit of butter smeared on it.

SCENE EIGHTEEN: ENCORE DINNER

In the restaurant.

KATHERINE and FREDDIE are at a table.

The ENTITY is still with them.

KATHERINE: Feel like salad or entree?

FREDDIE: I'm kind of hungry. Do they have that noodle thing?

KATHERINE: Think so.

FREDDIE: I'll have that. How was your day?

KATHERINE: Hard. I'm tired.

FREDDIE: Wait. What's the soup?

KATHERINE: Black bean.

FREDDIE: I'll have that.

KATHERINE: Did you go to the library today and get signed up?

FREDDIE: No. I went, but I can't just sign up. I have to get a medical form filled out.

KATHERINE: Oh, did you bring it with you?

FREDDIE: No. Look, it doesn't matter. I need a doctor to sign it anyway, so it's going to take a while.

KATHERINE: Well, I can help you if you want.

FREDDIE: No, there's really nothing you can do. I just have to put the date on it or something.

KATHERINE: Oh.

Pause.

FREDDIE: I wiped out on the steps when I was leaving. Can you see a bruise here?

KATHERINE: Yeah.

FREDDIE: Is it bad?

KATHERINE: Yeah.

FREDDIE: You didn't say anything.

KATHERINE: No.

FREDDIE: Okay.

KATHERINE: What am I going to say?

FREDDIE: Oh, I don't know. How about; "Why don't you use your cane?" "Why don't you be more careful?" "Why don't you get a guide dog?" "Why don't you get a little volunteer from the CNIB?" Why don't YOU finish your thesis?

KATHERINE: Do you want wine?

FREDDIE: Yeah.

KATHERINE: Red?

FREDDIE: Sure.

KATHERINE: A half litre, then, 'cause I'll have some too.

KATHERINE turns to find a waiter.

SCENE NINETEEN: SHRINK

In DR. SONDRA's office.

The ENTITY appears behind the scrim and mirrors DR. SONDRA.

FREDDIE: I, ah, thought it was time to get some support, and deal with some of the, um, inside stuff. I guess, I, well, there's not a lot of, I mean, you know, my mother, and um . . . I do swim a lot.

DR. SONDRA: You'd like to have an appointment.

FREDDIE: Yeah, that would be good. I'd like to come weekly.

DR. SONDRA: Or more if necessary. Mondays and Wednesdays at three?

FREDDIE: Good, fine.

SCENE TWENTY: DINING, WINING, AND RUNNING

At the restaurant.

The ENTITY *watches* KATHERINE *and* FREDDIE *at the table.*

KATHERINE: Aren't you going to eat something?

FREDDIE: No.

Pause.

KATHERINE: Has the library called you yet with the books?

FREDDIE: Yup. This wine tastes funny. Here, taste it.

She gives it to KATHERINE.

KATHERINE: Tastes all right to me. It's not like it's a twelve-dollar glass.

FREDDIE: Hmmm. Tastes funny to me.

KATHERINE: Do you want to send it back?

FREDDIE: No.

KATHERINE: Would you like my beer instead?

FREDDIE: No, keep your beer. Why should you drink skanky wine?

KATHERINE: I don't find it skanky.

FREDDIE: It's skanky.

KATHERINE: What books did you order?

SMUDGE | 45

FREDDIE: One Charles Dickens, a children's book. Some Canadian plays.

KATHERINE: That's great. When do you get them?

FREDDIE: I've got them already.

KATHERINE: Are they good?

FREDDIE: I don't know. Not really, I mean, it's someone else's voice. It's not like it's reading.

KATHERINE: Maybe you'll get used to it.

FREDDIE: I think there's cork in my glass.

KATHERINE: Let's see—no, I don't see anything.

FREDDIE: How was your baseball game?

KATHERINE: It was fun. We lost, of course, but it didn't matter. I hit a homer.

FREDDIE: Great. And you had your film class last night?

KATHERINE: Yeah, we watched *Bringing Up Baby*.

FREDDIE: Great! I hear that's funny.

KATHERINE: It's so funny! I'm not sure if you'd like it though; it's quite visual.

FREDDIE: Well, I'm sure I would like it if I could see it. I'm not sure I'm going to come over Sunday.

KATHERINE: I bought large-print cards so you could play.

FREDDIE: Oh, well, that was kind. Thank you. I just don't think I'm going to feel like playing cards on Sunday.

KATHERINE: How do you know? It's Tuesday.

FREDDIE: Um, I think I'll feel like, um, maybe taking a bus somewhere out of town for the day.

KATHERINE: Where are you going to go?

FREDDIE: Wawa, I think, Wawa, maybe, or Puslinch. I like Puslinch.

KATHERINE: Do you know the place?

FREDDIE: I've driven through it years ago. It's small, historical.

KATHERINE: And the bus goes there.

FREDDIE: I think there's a GO train.

KATHERINE: Even better.

SCENE TWENTY-ONE: SHRINK II

At DR. SONDRA's office.

The ENTITY appears behind the scrim and mirrors DR. SONDRA.

FREDDIE: It has nothing to do with my sight.

DR. SONDRA: Well, you seem quite anxious about something.

FREDDIE: I'm just thinking I have a hard time with commitment. I like things to be what they are, not some contract, you know, sign here on the dotted line.

DR. SONDRA: That sounds like a trap.

FREDDIE: Yes, yes, I guess so.

DR. SONDRA: Is it possible that someone might be in that position with you without feeling trapped?

FREDDIE: They can always leave if they want to. I don't expect anyone to commit to me, not now anyway.

DR. SONDRA: Why not now?

FREDDIE: Because I'm going blind. Someday I won't be going blind, I'll just be blind, and then it'll be okay.

DR. SONDRA: What will be okay?

FREDDIE: To commit to me. Once I'm blind, it'll be over.

DR. SONDRA: What will be over?

SCENE TWENTY-TWO: IN A DINER

FREDDIE sits and listens.

FREDDIE: The waitress clanks down ashtrays. Clicking lighter behind to my left. Busy eaters and, "there you go." Not much talking in here. A radio blares. Shuffling of feet. An elderly man—homeless, maybe? Money crunches. It even sounds cold. How many times can one person sniffle during one meal? How many sniffles can you detect in one room? Velcro. The Cadillac of goofy sounds. The older ladies are gathering for tea in the upper left corner. I decide to take a peek. Silhouettes. Shapes blurring the window light and nothing more. The world is becoming an old photograph right before my eyes. The ladies' voices are so full, so rich with history and detail. "I'm schtarvin' Edna, just schtarvt." Beauty basks in the comfy schmooch of these overly soft leather benches. Mid-afternoon. My favourite muffin. Ecstasy lives.

The lights fade.

FREDDIE sits in the middle of the space. A TECHNICIAN stands behind her.

SCENE TWENTY-THREE: A HOSPITAL ROOM

With the TECHNICIAN.

TECHNICIAN: Look at this picture. Tell me what you see.

FREDDIE does not look.

FREDDIE: Oh no. A bunch of dots?

TECHNICIAN: Look at the picture.

Pause.

FREDDIE looks.

FREDDIE: Smudge. I don't even see the dots anymore.

SCENE TWENTY-FOUR: THE BLIND ENTITY

FREDDIE stands centre stage, tapping with her cane as though walking.

The ENTITY appears with cane and dark glasses upstage of the scrim, facing and looking into the mirror, tapping her cane as she walks upstage.

The ENTITY *stops.*

FREDDIE *and the* ENTITY *wave their arms slowly up and down.*

FREDDIE: When I look in the mirror, I have to wave at myself so that the image of my hand can guide my eyes to see my face. Sometimes I look and see myself, then realize it's the lampshade.

I remember feeling heavy. Now I feel invisible. I look as if I've been blown apart. One day I will look and my image will be gone.

They wave to each other, waving to see if they can see their reflection in the mirror; waving to see if they can see their hand in front of their face. The waving becomes quicker, urgent.

The ENTITY *begins to leave, walking upstage and disappearing into the mirror and into the darkness.*

FREDDIE *is left alone, waving frantically to nobody.*

SCENE TWENTY-FIVE: SHRINK III

At DR. SONDRA*'s office.*

The ENTITY *appears behind the scrim and mirrors* DR. SONDRA.

DR. SONDRA: How did you make out with the antidepressants?

FREDDIE: Not very well.

DR. SONDRA: What happened?

FREDDIE: Well, you gave me drugs for the sadness and drugs to make me sleep.

DR. SONDRA: The antidepressants can give you sleep disorders.

FREDDIE: Yes, and at the same time I was taking antibiotics for an infection.

DR. SONDRA: Well, that shouldn't be a problem.

FREDDIE: No, except when you mix them all up and take the wrong dosage of everything when you think it's something else!

DR. SONDRA: Well, why would you do that?

FREDDIE: Because I can't see!

The ENTITY now crosses upstage of the scrim into shadow.

I overdosed on Prozac, I under-dosed on the sleeping pills. I completely forgot to take the antibiotics at all! I landed in emergency after collapsing in a big twitching sweat! As for the infection, well, let's not even go there!

DR. SONDRA: I suppose now you're going to think drugs are bad, won't try anymore.

The ENTITY returns mirroring DR. SONDRA.

FREDDIE: Yeah, right, forget it.

DR. SONDRA: You had a bad experience because you didn't take the time to organize yourself. You didn't have to mix up your pills.

FREDDIE: No, I didn't have to mix up my pills, but I did.

DR. SONDRA: You can't help yourself until you're feeling better.

FREDDIE: I don't want them, for fuck's sake! Oops. For heaven's sake.

Speaking simultaneously.

DR. SONDRA: You can swear in here.

THE ENTITY: You can say "fuck."

FREDDIE: Oh. Thank you. Fuck.

SCENE TWENTY-SIX: HI THERE. FUCK YOU

FREDDIE is at home on the phone, leaving a voicemail.

FREDDIE: Hello, doctor? I am leaving you a message and I would prefer that you don't return my call. Thank you for the time you've given me. I've decided that our therapy relationship has come to an impasse and I don't see the point in continuous conflict over what is best for me. I'm cancelling my next week's appointment and I will not be making anymore. Goodbye.

Pause.

She told me I could swear in her office. Maybe I should have said, "Hi there. Fuck you."

SCENE TWENTY-SEVEN: POSITIVE THINKING

The ENTITY lifts FREDDIE up onto one shoulder.

FREDDIE: Ladies and gentlemen of the House-and-Garden Positive-Thinking Society, how honoured I am that you have asked me here today to speak on the power of positive thinking and how it has affected my journey of loss. I'd like to begin by saying that losing your sight positively sucks. I think this. I'm positive about it. It's absolute, positive shite. Thank you. Any questions? Good.

Blackout.

In the dark a voice shouts, "Look out!"

SCENE TWENTY-EIGHT: IN FREDDIE'S ROOM

KATHERINE *stands.*

FREDDIE *lies in bed, under the duvet.*

The ENTITY *crouches behind her, holding onto the bed, which she moves for* FREDDIE *throughout the scene.*

KATHERINE: Three hundred dollars. I just spent three hundred dollars on this weekend and now you don't want to go!

FREDDIE: Sorry.

KATHERINE: What is wrong with you?! You've wanted to get out of the city for weeks. We picked this weekend. I go. I get a car. I take time off work and now you've changed your mind!

FREDDIE: I didn't change my mind.

KATHERINE: Last week you wanted to go, today you don't. I would say that's changing your mind.

FREDDIE: It's not my mind! I think you should go without me.

KATHERINE: Okay, just get out of bed, put your shoes on. Right there. Right there!

FREDDIE *puts her shoes on, then goes back to bed.*

Freddie, get up!

KATHERINE *grabs her arm*

FREDDIE: No!! Stand back, please.

FREDDIE *pulls away.*

KATHERINE: Okay, I'm back. About two feet to your left.

FREDDIE: I was trying to do something nice for you. I went to the IGA. I wanted to surprise you. Now it's all over Bathurst St. I was walking home up Bathurst carrying all these bags of stuff. Little baby corns for the spinach salad. A Bundt cake. A voice yelled, "Look out!" like, really loud.

ENTITY *shouts "look out" with* FREDDIE.

"LOOK OUT!" I jumped. It startled me. The bags went flying. The tomatoes started rolling across the sidewalk. I just start grabbing them. The voice yells—

ENTITY *yells with* FREDDIE.

"YOU'RE ON THE STREET!" So I drop everything—the mushrooms and the Pet Rock magazine I bought for us—and then I realize I'm not on the street, I'm on the sidewalk. So, I just sort of stand there and say, "Asshole!" I try to find the mushroom bag, but I can't find it. So I give up and just keep walking. About a block later I hear him again. And this time, I catch a glimpse of his coat, circling me. I can see him because he's on the outside, running ahead and circling. I turn, put my cane in the air and I tell him, "I'll beat the shit out of you if you come anywhere near me again." Half a block later, there he is again, hiding behind something on the sidewalk. Now, that's the boy nearly dead at this point—I stand there and I contemplate how I will kill him with my cane.

KATHERINE: So, what happened?

Back in bed.

FREDDIE: I ducked into a store and tricked him into thinking I was crossing the road.

KATHERINE: So he was gone after that?

FREDDIE: Yeah, I guess so. Right now, I hate everybody, and in this condition I think it's best for everybody if I remain still, under a duvet, unstartled.

KATHERINE: Would you like some tea?

FREDDIE: I would like some tea.

KATHERINE: Would you like an Arrowroot cookie?

FREDDIE: I would like an Arrowroot cookie.

SCENE TWENTY-NINE: THE DARK THIEF

FREDDIE sits in the dark

The ENTITY explores FREDDIE's face with a light.

FREDDIE: It's waiting for me. Lurking in the shadows. It's waiting for me to stop. Stop feeling, stop caring, stop wanting, stop loving. It would have me shrink. I can't escape it. It's inside of me.

FREDDIE catches a glimpse of the ENTITY.

Suddenly, the lights go off.

FREDDIE *crawls across the floor in the darkness to find her coat. She stands and puts it on.*

SCENE THIRTY: ESCAPE FROM THE DARK THIEF

The Dyke Bar. Dance music blares.

FREDDIE *alone with her cane at centre. She is nauseous, she stumbles, she collapses.*

SCENE THIRTY-ONE: THE LIGHT BEARER

FREDDIE *at a new* THERAPIST'*s office (played by the* ENTITY*).*

THERAPIST: I'm a little concerned about your reason for coming here. Your message said that your friend wanted you to come. When I hear that, I hear, "I don't really want to be here."

FREDDIE: You have good hearing.

THERAPIST: So why are you here?

FREDDIE: I don't know. My life. It's not a bad life. I loved my life.

THERAPIST: And now you're blind.

FREDDIE: Look, I'm not blind. I can see. Differently than you, but I can see.

THERAPIST: Yes. Quite differently. I'm a total.

FREDDIE: A total what?

THERAPIST: Blind. I'm totally blind.

56 | INTERDEPENDENT MAGIC

Long pause. FREDDIE *cries.*

The Kleenex is down to your right.

SCENE THIRTY-TWO: FREDDIE'S ROOM

It is quite dark.

FREDDIE *pulls papers and pencil from her knapsack and writes frantically in very large letters, a word per page.*

With each word, the ENTITY, *upstage of the scrim, holds a card to the light.*

DEAR
GOD
WHAT
ARE
YOU
FUCKING
THINKING.

KATHERINE *appears dimly behind the scrim.*

KATHERINE: Freddie?

FREDDIE: *(suddenly)* I need to not see you so much.

Pause. It grows darker.

KATHERINE: Can you see my face?

FREDDIE: No. The light is too dark.

KATHERINE: Do you know that I'm crying?

FREDDIE: No, it's not in your voice. In the dark, I don't even know if you're still there. In fact, maybe you've quietly slipped away.

Pause.

You see, you didn't say anything just now and I don't even know if you're there.

Pause.

Is your face all squished up in horror. It is, isn't it.

Pause.

It would be nice if you would tell me. I can't see, you know!

KATHERINE: Shut up! Just shut up! If you could see me, you would know. You'd see the look on my face. You'd see my eyes and you would know. I'm sorry I don't have the words.

KATHERINE leaves.

FREDDIE sits alone.

Night is falling.

FREDDIE scrambles round the room, picks up the papers, puts on her coat, and gathers her things.

The ENTITY has entered the room and stops her from leaving.

They struggle.

The ENTITY, with great strength, pushes FREDDIE to the ground.

Finally, FREDDIE *surrenders. In the darkness we hear a cry of pain.*

The ENTITY *places her hand on* FREDDIE'S *head.*

The ENTITY *exits.*

FREDDIE *is left lying on the floor.*

The lights slowly brighten from here to the end of the play.

SCENE THIRTY-THREE: A DIFFERENT HOSPITAL

FREDDIE *wakens in a white room. There is a big window, which fills the room with light.*

The NURSES *appear upstage of the scrim.*

NURSE 1: Hello, Frederica. How are you feeling this morning?

FREDDIE: Fine.

NURSE 1: You haven't come out of your room for several days.

FREDDIE: Oh.

NURSE 1: Can you spell world backwards?

FREDDIE: D L R . . .

NURSE 2: Hello, Freddie. How are you feeling this morning?

FREDDIE: Fine, thank you.

NURSE 2: Are you attending the seminar this afternoon? We're making fridge magnets at four.

FREDDIE: No, thank you.

NURSE 2: You haven't eaten in several days. Are you seeing things?

NURSE 1: Freddie, the police are coming to take you to our seminar. Fridge magnets at four.

FREDDIE: I don't need fridge magnets. I don't put little notes on my fridge anymore.

The NURSES leave.

FREDDIE stands, looks out of the window. She watches out of the window for quite a while.

SCENE THIRTY-FOUR: ELEGY

FREDDIE stands in front of the window.

FREDDIE: If I close my eyes and practice, practice feeling with my heart, my soul, my desire in the dark . . . If I practice and touch, practice and love, I can stay with the light.

The sun is warm.
It's always been warm.

My dear beloved sight.
You allowed me to feel freedom in my body. You protected me. You loved a clear goal and the passage forward. The five ball in the corner pocket, the end of the dirt path to the maple tree, the walk across the bar to the girl. Sight loved her best-friend's smile, the space between her grandmother's front teeth, the red ring left on cigarette butts. The morning sun on the crystal water, the laughing reflections in the sky. Sight drank the world in so deeply that no passing can ever erase it. You did not live long, but you did live well. In peace may you find new life.

FREDDIE hears geese flying overhead and sees them clearly with her ears. The ENTITY *watches the geese from upstage of the scrim.*

Look at the geese.

The lights fade to darkness.

End.

ACCESS ME

BY
THE BOYS IN CHAIRS COLLECTIVE
ANDREW GURZA
KEN HARROWER
FRANK HULL
DEBBIE PATTERSON
BRIAN POSTALIAN
AND
JONATHAN SEINEN

Dedicated to all those who make the world
more accessible
and
more queer.

ACKNOWLEDGEMENTS

We would like to express our gratitude to Marjorie Chan for inviting Ken into the Cahoots Theatre office that fateful day, and for Cahoots's invaluable support of the project. We'd like to thank Indrit Kasapi and Sarah Garton Stanley respectively for connecting us and transforming our collective from one to five and five to six.

This play is truly a labour of love, and we want to thank all the collaborators who have made this transition from personal conversation to performance text possible.

INTRODUCTION
BY JESSICA WATKIN

When I first experienced *Access Me*, which at the time in 2017 was called *Boys in Chairs*, I was quite nervous. I was nervous because I couldn't read the question card that was also my ticket. I was nervous because I was alone. I had come with a friend, but their need for ASL interpretation meant facing an open window with light coming in and I couldn't face that direction. Even in a Disability performance there were competing needs as audience members. After the show (the performers didn't ask me to read them a question; I unclenched immediately after that section passed!) I knew that this was a special kind of performance.

They were doing something *different* here, and that was exciting.

I've had the privilege of experiencing this performance multiple times as it has evolved, and I am intrigued by the co-creation methods, vulnerability, and interdependence present. Each performer supports the others in those moments of vulnerability. Each team member brings their perspective and lived experience of the world to the table. This is a play about Disability and queer sexuality in Canada from the perspective of three gay/queer wheelchair-using men, with engaging stagecraft and shifts in audience perspective that generate feelings and questions about how Disabled gay/queer men in Canada are seen and presented in non-performance spaces. I find myself comparing my own Disability and queer experiences with theirs, finding crossroads where they diverge from my knowledge, and clocking when I am learning about new experiences. The three performers use different ways of engaging with the audience to slip between tone: at the top, the tone is cordial and inviting, like new friends! Audience members are greeted enthusiastically and invited into the space. The tone continues to shift as the performance progresses: educational when talking about the realities of being Disabled and requiring support; flirtatious at times when the content pivots to turn-ons and sexier topics; and confessional when each performer reveals their internal explorations of sexuality and self. I find the tonal shifts contribute to the magic of the piece. The shifts ask the audience to reposition themselves in relationship to the performers: as a friend, as a peer, as an ally, as a confidant, and as a lover. By inviting the audience into their world, the characters of *Access Me* allow a controlled environment for accessing *them*.

Each performer showcases their strengths in this piece and also has built some kind of support into the structure and text. There is a "friend-tendant" noted in the text, which Christine Kelly identifies in her essay "Building Bridges With Accessible Care: Disability Studies, Feminist Care Politics, and Beyond" as a nuanced relationship of care with friends where the lines may be blurred between what is *friendship* and what is *support worker support*.[1] These kinds of relationships are plentiful in Disabled lives, and the acknowledgement of this relationship in the text is a good reminder that although *Access Me i*s performed by three men, the productions are possible because of teams of friend-tendants behind or in front of the scenes. What this role, the "friend-tendant," offers and emphasizes in this performance (and beyond) is a way to negotiate care when the guidelines aren't clear because of loving relationships where dignity and kindness exist. (I'm thinking here of Andrew's beautiful moments of audience participation, when he asks an audience member to perform the acts of his support worker, but engage with him as a lover would). What this play reveals about care and love is that it isn't as direct or as obvious, as we may expect.

The text is deeply personal and unique to the team, but also very specific to the performers. Frank Hull, Andrew Gurza, and Ken Harrower infused this performance with their lives, love, curiosity, pain, grief, and so much more that this text cannot readily be picked up by other hands. It would seem disingenuous for anyone else to perform a song such as "Small foot man" or to deliver Frank's incredible monologue to his ex-lover Enrico. What follows is not so much a blueprint for others

---

[1] Kelly, Christine. "Building Bridges with Accessible Care: Disability Studies, Feminist Care Scholarship, and Beyond," *A Journal of Feminist Philosophy* 28, no. 4 (Fall 2013): 784–800. https://doi.org/10.1111/j.1527-2001.2012.01310.x.

to perform, as it is a record of a performance that took place in the past and exists as an archive. I suggest that you, dear reader, take from this performance their co-creative practice, the engaging vulnerability, and the strong Disability pride in these pages.

Access Me starts and finishes in an upbeat, joyful, and inviting way with music and dancing. As an audience member of this piece, being asked questions and moving around to co-create the space with the performers, you feel a part of the action. While experiencing this piece in a different way, on the page, I encourage you to imagine comfort. Imagine three charismatic and kind performers smiling and introducing themselves to you. Imagine dancing with strangers in soft and silly ways. Imagine being nervous to ask a question, perform, offer an anecdote, but having that nervousness immediately melt away when the performers approach you to contribute, because they are all comforting presences that put you at ease. Imagine learning so much about queer Disabled sexuality that you want to learn more. Imagine leaving the performance, head bopping along with the music, and holding that magic feeling for a few days. I hope this text brings you a piece of the joy and strength of the performance it represents.

> *This is a sexually explicit performance, and readers should know prior to reading that there are moments that re-enact and speak frankly about sex. Although not explicitly violent, there are descriptions of traumatic and non-consensual encounters. Therefore, please consider your current personal state prior to reading this piece as it may be triggering due to its explicit nature.*

Access Me was first presented as *Boys in Chairs* in Toronto at the SummerWorks Performance Festival on August 7, 2017, as part of the Lab Series, with the financial support of the Toronto Arts Council, the Ontario Arts Council through Creators Reserve Grants via Cahoots Theatre and Tangled Arts and a direct grant, a Community One Rainbow Grant, and it featured the following creative team:

Performers: Andrew Gurza, Ken Harrower, and Frank Hull
Director: Jonathan Seinen
Associate Director: Brian Postalian
Dramaturge: Debbie Patterson
Choreographer: Frank Hull
Stage Manager: Kjell Cawsey

The performers were awarded the inaugural Jon Kaplan Spotlight Award.

Subsequently, *Access Me* was presented by Boys in Chairs Collective as a Production Workshop at the Pia Bouman School for Ballet and Creative Movement in Toronto on July 13 and 14, 2019, with the financial support of the Canada Council for the Arts, the Ontario Arts Council, Cahoots Theatre, and Inside Out Theatre, and it featured the following creative team:

Performers: Andrew Gurza, Ken Harrower, and Frank Hull
Director: Jonathan Seinen
Associate Director: Brian Postalian
Dramaturge: Debbie Patterson
Choreographer: Frank Hull
Stage Manager: Aidan Morishita-Miki
Scenography (Set/Props/Lighting) Designer: Michelle Tracey

Costume Designer: Laura Delchiaro
Video Designers: Kyle Duffield and Madison Cooke
Sound Designer/Composer: Johnny Salib
Design Consultants: Audrey-Anne Bouchard and Jan Derbyshire
Assistant Designer/Associate Producer/Personal Support Worker: Jordan Campbell
Production Manager/Technical Director: Jayson McLean
Producers: Yousef Kadoura and Jonathan Seinen

Boys in Chairs Collective was an artist-in-residence with Cahoots Theatre, 2017 to 2020.

Andrew

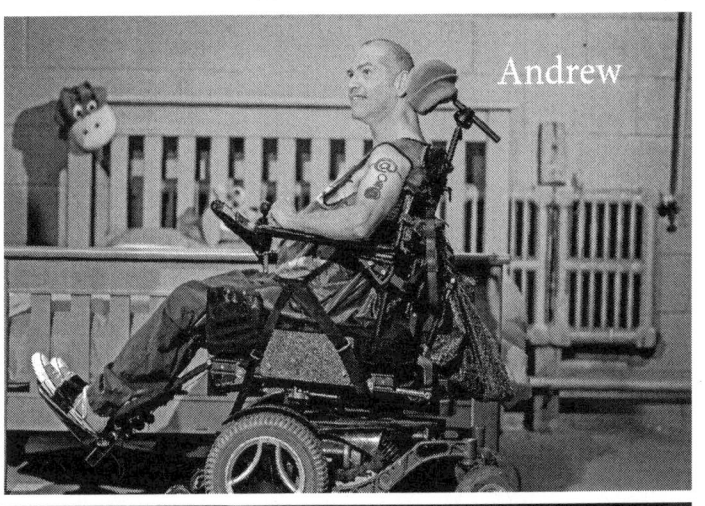

Frank

Ken

The experience begins as the audience checks in at the box office. They are given a Question Card and are told to hold on to it until the start of the performance. (The full list of questions is at the end of the script as an appendix.) As they move from the foyer into the performance space, they are met by an attendant ("friend-tendant" as we like to say). If the audience member is arriving already seated, the attendant will invite them to find a spot to settle in around the perimeter of the space. If they are arriving on foot, the attendant will offer a chair and invite the audience member to find a spot around the perimeter. In addition to addressing the basic access needs of the non-seated audience members by providing chairs, the attendant will also offer to carry the chair to wherever the audience member would like it to be should they be unable to carry it themselves.

The performers greet the audience as they enter the performance space. They introduce themselves informally and introduce audience members to each other as they encourage conversation. The audience, once seated, leave four "doorways" at the corners for the actors to enter and exit through or to hang out in when they want to join the audience circle. The audience will have to adjust to accommodate each other as more people arrive, collaborating to create access for everyone. In this spirit, one at a time, the audience creates the seating area together. The atmosphere is intimate, adaptive, and a bit chaotic.

Once everyone has been seated, ANDREW *commands our attention.* FRANK *and* KEN *each tuck into one of the doorways.*

ANDREW: Hi. Hello! Hi, everyone.

72 | INTERDEPENDENT MAGIC

> *It takes a bit of effort to bring order to this lively encounter. Once it is achieved,* ANDREW *takes the centre of the performance space.*

Welcome, welcome, thank you for coming! My name is Andrew Gurza, and I'm a disability awareness consultant. I'm your Number One Queer Cripple. My hobbies are podcasting, presenting, and porn. I love '80s pop and bad Chinese food. I'm a Disabled Dork With A Big Dick.

> ANDREW *wheels out in a wide arc to move into one of the doorways as* FRANK *swoops into centre stage.*

FRANK: I'm a horny gimp with a really big . . .

> *He presses in his belly to try to see his groin, but, alas, he cannot.*

. . . belly. I can't see my dick anymore. My name is Frank. I'm a choreographer and a dancer and also an up-and-coming actor. I'm learning as I go. And I'm the romantic of the group.

> FRANK *glides romantically into one of the doorways as* KEN *presses forward.*

KEN: Hello, my name is Ken. I'm an artist and actor, but mostly an actor. I have what is called Arthrogryposis Multiplex Congenita, or AMC. And, I have a *biiiiiiiiig* foot fetish. And my hobbies are: I like to read, watch TV, and go to the movies. I'm the horny one of the group, but also . . . the bitch.

> FRANK *and* ANDREW *join* KEN *centre stage.*

ANDREW: So, when you came in, each of you was given a card. Could you pull them out now? On the cards are questions we as disabled men get asked all the time about our sexuality, our disabilities, our day-to-day. And we want to get these questions out of the way right away so we can get to the meatier part of the show. Pun intended!

ANDREW pulls up to an audience member.

So . . . Hello. Hi, I'm Andrew.

ANDREW laughs at himself.

But you probably know that already. What's your name?

The audience member answers.

Can you please read the question on your card?

Usually this is met with discomfort. Sometimes the audience member says, "Do I have to?" or "I'd really rather not, it's so mean," to which the performers reply with a positive attitude, comforting the audience that it's okay, that they were the ones who wrote the questions. This part of the performance is different every time, and the following section is a record of the performance from July 14, 2019.

With adequate coaxing, the audience member reads their card.

Thank you for that question! The question is, "How do you go to the bathroom?"

And my answer is: I'm kind of like royalty, so I have people do that for me.

KEN: I'm able to do it on my own. I pull down my pants, hop onto the toilet, do what I do, and I'm done.

FRANK: Well, my bathroom is accessible so I transfer, do my business. But I'm really hairy so I transfer to the tub. Make sure I'm nice and washed, if you know what I mean.

It's my turn to pick a victim. Who's my victim?

FRANK spins in his chair with an index finger pointing straight ahead. When he stops, whichever person he finds himself pointing to is the person he approaches.

Oh, do you have a card?

Of course they do! The audience member asks the question.

Oooo, that's a good question. The question is, "What turns you on?"

Kissing turns me on the most. Yeah.

ANDREW: I like a lot of chest hair, a lot of muscles; I like a lot of ginger-bearded people . . . so, yeah, that's what turns me on.

KEN: Me? I like hairy guys. And, yeah—big feet: long and wide. Thank you for the question. So, who is our next victim . . .

KEN scans the room looking for someone to pick on.

—You!

The audience member asks the question.

The question is, "If I date you, will I have to be your attendant?"

No, I'm able to do most everything on my own, but once in a while I do like to be helped.

ANDREW: Yeah, you might have to help me out a little bit. I have attendant care workers for some of the other stuff I can't do, but, yeah, you might have to help me out with a few things. And that's going to be okay.

FRANK: I don't really need an attendant. I can do most things by myself. But if it's to my benefit, like getting my attendant on the train for free or stuff like that, I kind of use it to my advantage. Kind of like a really unethical disability.

KEN: Okay, the next victim? You, ma'am.

The audience member asks the question.

Oh! A good one! "How do I flirt with you?"

For me? Just be nice, and caring and show me some love. And also, maybe some feet.

ANDREW: How do you flirt with me? You could get down on one knee, you could touch my earlobe, whisper in my ear . . . Stuff like that.

FRANK cannot pass up an opportunity to flirt, so he moves up close to an audience member.

FRANK: I have this line that I use if I want someone to come home. And the line is, "If we are what we eat, I could be you by morning."

Sometimes an audience member says, "What did you say? I couldn't hear you." And the performers adjust accordingly. For instance, FRANK will turn himself around, pull in even closer, slowly and intimately repeating his answer: "If we are what we eat . . . I could be YOU by morning."

ANDREW: Thank you for that question.

ANDREW approaches another guest.

Hello. Could you read the question on your card?

They do.

The question is, "What is my type?" And I'll repeat: Ginger, chest hair, beautiful, that's my type. But also, a nice person, that's my type too.

KEN: He has to be tall, hairy, big hands, and yeah, big feet.

FRANK: I don't really have a specific type anymore. I tend to stay in the moment with somebody I like. I know I have the ability to feel passion and love for somebody no matter what their shape is or how old they get. The depth of the passion is love.

Another victim here.

The audience asks the question.

Yes. The question was, "Are there any kinks and fetishes we can explore together?" "Together"? Do you mean ALL of us together?

FRANK is now flirting with the ENTIRE audience!

Oh, oh, oh, oh, I have the most boring fetish of all: I have a suit-and-tie fetish, and I'd peel them off with my mouth.

ANDREW: That would take some time.

KEN: Oh, yeah, I have many kinks and fetishes, but I hope by now you know what one of them is. I've only said it four times now. I also like hairy guys, big guys, and small hairy guys, too, but mostly big hairy guys and we'll see where it goes from there.

ANDREW: Just like Ken I've said my fetishes many times today. Ginger hair, beard, and muscles. And also: if you want to know my fetishes, see me after the show.

FRANK: Thank you for asking those awkward questions, you've been an awesome audience. You're also a very good-looking audience, so fantastic in every way.

FRANK approaches an audience member.

And I want to wear you as a hat.

And another.

And you as a hat.

And another.

And you as a hat . . .

FRANK's impulse to flirt is completely out of control. He must be stopped. Thankfully ANDREW and KEN intervene and chase FRANK offstage.

ANDREW & KEN: All right! Okay! Bye, bye, bye, off you go. That's enough.

Once FRANK is subdued and moves to one of the corner doorways, KEN yields the floor to ANDREW.

ANDREW: Such a flirt. As you saw, we get asked pretty awkward questions about our day. My day's a little bit different because I need attendant care, which means that every morning before 8:00 a.m., someone comes to my room to get me out of bed. A lot of you might not have any experience of this kind of thing, but what if I gave you some?

ANDREW approaches an audience member.

Hi there.

They greet him back.

Can you say, "Good morning, Andrew"?

They do.

Perfect! You said that as coldly and impersonally as my attendant care worker does. Now this time, I'd like you to say, "Good morning, Andrew," but I'd like you to say it as if we're lovers.

They do.

Mmmmmm. One more time?

They do. Most passionately.

Wow. Thank you!

ANDREW *takes centre stage again.*

After I get up, it's time for me to go for a shower. When I'm in the shower I get washed by my attendant care worker. So . . .

ANDREW *approaches a different guest, getting very close.*

Hi. I'm going to cast you as my attendant care worker and you have to give me a shower. And we're going to use my arm as a prop. I want you to pretend like you only have five minutes to shower me and you have five other people to get up. And how would you do that?

They do, rubbing his arm roughly.

That's amazing. This time though, I want you to pretend like . . .

ANDREW *can't help but laugh at himself at the awkwardness of the situation.*

. . . like we're lovers and you're going to shower with me. Wanna try that with me?

They do, rubbing his arm much more sensually.

Niiiiice. Thank you.

ANDREW *again takes centre stage.*

After the shower, I go about my day: I do some podcast prep; I do some presentation prep; I listen to some Adele; I cry my heart out; and awesome things like that. And then, about three times a day I have to be catheterized to go pee, which I lovingly refer to as being "stabbed in the dick." So . . .

ANDREW *approaches another guest. They are terrified, contemplating what they might be asked to do!*

Hi! Do you think you want to help me cath—

ANDREW *senses their fear.*

No, no, just kidding!

ANDREW *skedaddles back to centre stage.*

After that I do some more podcast prep, I have some dinner, I see some friends, and go on the Internet looking for some D sometimes, that kind of stuff . . .

And then it's time for bed. So . . .

ANDREW *approaches another guest.*

Hello. Can you say, "Good night, Andrew"?

They do.

80 | INTERDEPENDENT MAGIC

Perfect, you said it really efficiently and properly just like my attendant care workers do. Thank you so much. This time, though, I'd like you to say, "Good night, Andrew," but I'd like you to say it like we are about to go to bed together. How would you say that?

> *They do, more gently this time.*

You know . . . I'm not really feeling the passion that I want to feel. We are so close, but just not there yet.

One more time. Here, I'll get in really close to you.

So, okay, now how would you say it?

> *ANDREW has moved in really close to the audience member. They repeat, "Good night, Andrew," this time with great passion. ANDREW pauses.*

I mean . . . It's just not quite there yet, but we're sooooo close.

One more time for me and, if it helps, if you are able to stand up, maybe give me a hug or a kiss, if that will help you . . .

Now how would you say, "Good night, Andrew"?

> *They do, embracing ANDREW, looking deep into his eyes and caressing his hair.*

Awww, nice. Thank you. Thank you very much for being part of my disabled day.

> *ANDREW wheels off to one of the doorways and KEN slowly comes out, commanding our attention.*

KEN: Alan.

I met Alan on a nice warm hot
hot sunny day in June.
It was a couple of weeks before my twenty-fifth birthday. Oh boy!
And I'm lonely, so I go out for a spin and I end up in a park.
And I don't know anybody in the park.

But I notice Alan.
He's sitting on a bench,
I happen to notice he has big hands
and big feet.
I'm checking him out. But I don't stare at him.

I see him look around, and then I finally get up the nerve and I go over
to Alan.
And I say, "Hi."
Then he says, "Hi."
We start talking and then I ask him:
"Sometime, how would you like to come over?"
And he says, "Sure."
Then I ask, "Have you ever had a foot massage?"
"Oh yeah."
"Aw, nice."
So, I ask him for his phone number, I offer him mine, and we
part ways.

Then a couple of weeks later . . .
It's my birthday!
I turned twenty-five.
And I'm at home,
and I'm bored,
and I'm horny.
I remember Alan and I find his phone number.

I call him.

"Hello. Hey, hey, Alan. It's Ken . . . Yeah, it is nice to hear you, too . . . Hey, are you busy today? No? How would you like to come over for a bit? . . . Okay! . . . In about forty-five minutes? Okay, bye."

Forty-five minutes pass.

    KEN *knocks on the arm of his chair.*

"Yeah, come on in, it's open.
And take off your shoes by the door, please."

We head over to the couch.
I hop out of my chair onto the couch and I ask him,
"May I give you a foot massage?"
And he says,
"Okay, sure."
So, I ask him to put his feet on my knees.

And I take
off
his
socks.

Ahhhhh, nice big feet!

Mmmmm nice.
And I start to do a foot massage.
I'm hoping he'll start to fall asleep.
And he does.
But then I start to have a boner.

Oh no.

And then I think, *Oh, no, I don't want him to . . . I hope he doesn't wake up.*

Okay, he's fallen asleep.
So I slowly move his foot
onto my cock
and start to massage it.
And I'm thinking,
Please don't wake up,
because I don't want him to get mad and leave.

And he starts to wake up.
Oh no.
Oh crap.
I don't want him to get mad.

And he asks me,
"What are you doing?"

"I'm sorry, I have a foot fetish, and feet turn me on."

And then he asks me,
"If you wanted to play around, why didn't you just ask me?"

"Well,
one: I don't know you,
two: I'm not out,
three: I thought you would get mad at me."

And then he turns it on me.
He asks, "Have you ever had a blow job?"

"No."

"Would you like to have a blow job?"

"Sure."

So I hop back into my chair, we go into the bedroom,

I hop onto the bed,
and he pulls down my pants
and he starts to suck
on my cock.
Ahhhhhhh, it feels good.

About fifteen minutes after, he asks me,
"Are you about to come?"

"Sorry, not yet."

    KEN holds a long pause.

Forty-five minutes later, I'm about ready to come.
"Slower . . . faster . . . slower! Faster!"

    KEN gasps.

AAAAAAAAAAHHHHHHHHHHHHHH!

And I come.
And it's my first openly gay experience.
And it's the best birthday present I've ever had.

    KEN glides blissfully into one of the doorways as ANDREW takes centre.

ANDREW: Close your eyes and harken back to 1999. Do you remember 1999? ICQ was a thing.

    ICQ sound effect.

Y2K was coming.

    Microsoft Windows launch sound effect.

Friends was still on the air.

The first chords of the Friends *theme song play.*

In 1999, I was fifteen. I was a huge nerd. I liked musicals like *Phantom of the Opera,* romantic comedies—actually, though, not much has changed. Also, when I was fifteen, I was in grade ten and there was a boy named Mike who I really, *really* liked—and I really wanted to do things to him. With my mouth. So much so that I even picked my class schedule to match up with his.

I decided that I wanted to sleep with him, and I came up with this elaborate plan. I was like, "I know what I'll do! I'll have to pee!"

Normally when I have to pee, I have an attendant care worker who comes, takes me into the washroom, pulls down my pants, and puts a urinal under my junk. But on this day, I would make sure there was no attendant around. So, in drama class, I drink a lot of water, I'm sipping and sipping. After class, I bump into Mike and say, "Hey, I really need to piss. Can you help me out?" And he looks around and he's like, "Uhhhhhhhh. Uhhhhhhh. Sure, man, no problem."

He said yes. Yay!

ANDREW executes a flawless pirouette of pure horny adolescent glee.

So there we were, walking in the hall. I'm in front and he's behind, so he can't see me smiling.

ANDREW rolls across the space re-enacting this moment of delicious anticipation.

I'm brimming with excitement about this encounter. He's going to pull down my pants and: See. My. Dick. And when he sees my dick, he's going to want to have sex with me, right there. He'll hop on my chair and blow me, and it'll be great!

86 | INTERDEPENDENT MAGIC

But just as this fantasy is about to go down for real in real life, the creepy vice-principal comes up and goes, "No, don't worry, Mike. I've got it, I'll help Andrew. It's no problem."

Sigh.

A few days later, on ICQ, I saw Mike and I said, "Hey man, I just want to thank you so much for helping me the other day, thanks a lot. And also . . . I want to let you know that I like you. And I'm wondering . . . Do you like me too?"

> ANDREW *looks at the audience, wondering, "Do you like me too?" No one answers him. He begins looking at his phone, chatting with guys online on Scruff, where his handle is* BDC *(Big Dick Cripple). The Scruff Chat window is projected above him, where guys say discriminatory and awful things to him. Eventually, there is a chat that seems to be going somewhere, this one with* GB *(Ginger Beef). Simultaneously,* FRANK *and* KEN *discuss the bars they used to visit in the '90s, in the former days of Toronto's gay village.*

FRANK: Hey, Ken, do you remember the hustler bar on Yonge Street called Sneakers?

Ginger Beef has shared their private album with you.

KEN: Oh, do I ever! I often hung out there, and I loved it because of all the cute guys. But it was a bitch to get in and out. And every time I had to go to the bathroom, I had to go down out of the door, with a step—yay, big—had to go to the hotel across the street, come back, go back up that step. It was a bitch! How about Traxx?

BDC
Hi. Whoa, you're hot.

You have just shared your private album with Ginger Beef.

FRANK: Traxx! The accessible entrance was through the rear. Yeah, all the good accessible doors are always through the rear. I remember Traxx. The dance floor was at the back as well.

KEN: Yeah, and the piano bar was in the front. And I often hung out there because in the back it was too crowded, too many people. I often hit on older, hairier, tall guys who had big feet.

Hey Andrew! How do you meet guys?

ANDREW: Mostly, I meet guys online—actually, I'm doing it right now!

FRANK: Well, there was this one leather bar outside the village on Eastern Avenue called the Toolbox. You really didn't have to worry about the bathroom not being accessible because they had a big bathtub in the middle of the bar . . .

And, well, all you leather boys know what that's about.

KEN: Oh, wow, okay, that's not my scene.

> GB
> Whoa, nice dick. Hey, what's up?

> BDC
> Wuuuuf.

> GB
> Thx for the wuuuf, stud.

> BDC
> Cool, man.

> GB
> So, what are you into?

FRANK: There was also a country and western bar called Badlands. And I used to watch the guys line dance. I really loved the way they'd thrust their crotches out and in and around.

> BDC
> Oral. Kissing. Topping. Rimming. You?

KEN: What? No way! There was an actual country gay bar? Oh, man! That was before my time. I wish I were here, but I didn't come to town until '99.

> GB
> Same. Vers top here.

FRANK: Yeah, I came here in '91, and at 5 St. Joseph Street there was this awesome dance club that was completely accessible called Colby's.

> BDC
> So, we should hang out sometime, bro.

KEN: Oh. I've heard of it, but that was before my time.

FRANK: And back in those days, you know, we did some funky dances. Yeah. Like the Funky Chicken.

> *FRANK demonstrates the move, jutting his head forward like a chicken pecking.*

And then the Fonze.

> *FRANK makes two thumbs-up and raises alternating hands from his waistband to his shoulder.*

And the Mashed Potato.

> FRANK *makes two fists, holding them in front of his body he brings the right fist down on the left and then the left fist down on the right, and repeats.*

And then the Fist Bump.

> FRANK *does a similar move to the Mashed Potato, this time sharing the action with audience members to the right and to the left of him.* ANDREW, *left hanging by* GB, *puts his phone away.* ANDREW *and* KEN *withdraw to the doorways, while* FRANK *takes centre stage.*

Ken! I'm going to teach this dance to the audience. I'm going to try to do it in fours. I'll probably make a ton of mistakes, but we're going to try to do it in fours. You shout out each move for me, okay? And we'll teach the audience.

> KEN *and* FRANK *show the dance moves: the Funky Chicken, the Fonze, the Mashed Potato, and the Fist Bump, isolating each move for the audience to try, and then teaching a sequence that cycles through them all, repeating each one four times.* KEN *calls out the moves and* FRANK *keeps count. The dance with the audience concludes, and* FRANK *is overcome by a reverie of Church Street in its heyday. The stage lights start shifting around him.*

Picture it. Church Street. 1991. It's summertime. The Second Cup is there with guys always hanging out on the steps. Otherwise known as the Suction Cup.

Can I get everyone who can stand to stand up, please?

> *They do.* FRANK *does a full turn in the middle of the audience as he points at each of them.*

As you wheel along Church Street, in your power chair, you notice every single hard-on through every guy's shorts. Mmmmm. What's a poor boy to do?

Thank you! You may all sit.

> *They do.*

Well, there is an accessible bathhouse called St. Mark's. I know, I'll go there.

> FRANK *re-enacts wheeling into the lobby of St. Mark's, right up to the elevator.*

I hit the elevator button and . . . The elevator's broken!

> *He heaves a sigh.*

Wow. I'm so horny, that the light from Horny will take two billion fucking years to reach the earth and *the bathhouse isn't accessible!* Okay, okay, I can handle this.

I'm going to Queen's Park. Queen's Park is always accessible.

> FRANK *wheels around in breathless anticipation of the pleasures that await at Queen's Park. The lights begin to dim.*

So, I arrive at Queen's Park and I observe the shadows. Moving. Pulsing. And I know exactly what they're doing.

And I move toward them and park.

> FRANK *parks in the centre of the playing space.*

And I notice that the shadows form a circle around me. Kind of like the circle that's around me now. And you know what happens? This is what happens. We start doing this dance. You know the dance . . .

Ken, I'm going to count them in again.

KEN: Yeah.

FRANK: Five, six—five, six, seven, eight!

> *With* FRANK *guiding them through the sequence and* KEN *calling out the changes, the audience dances.* FRANK *slowly begins to alter the moves . . . slowly . . . until he's giving blow jobs (the Funky Chicken), undoing his belt (the Fonze), masturbating (Mashed Potato), and giving hand jobs (Fist Bump).* KEN *begins to offer more instructions "Slower . . . Faster . . . " The dance becomes sensual; the dance becomes rhythmic.* FRANK *becomes ravenous and caught up in a frenzy. Suddenly,* FRANK *spins his chair around and hollers out the sound of a police siren. He freezes. Busted!*

Cop car. The men scatter. Lights shining on me. Shorts down to my ankles. My hard-on there for the whole world to see.

The cop walks up.

"Hi . . ."

> *He laughs nervously.*

" . . . Could you help me with my pants? . . . Please?"

> FRANK *re-enacts the moment: flirting with the cop pulling up his pants, and then trying to move—but the chair won't budge.*

"I'm stuck in the mud. Could you get your partner to come out of the car and help pull me out of the mud?"

> FRANK *rocks back and forth until he finally lurches forward. He hightails it out of there.*

I got away with it! I played the disability card and I won. BIG TIME!

> FRANK *begins to dance in celebration, to flowing romantic music. But his movement is impeded by the small space. He needs more room! He appeals to the audience.*

It's a shame that all these seats are in my way ... Could I ask for your help? Would you mind moving your chairs to just over there?

> *They oblige, and the space changes from having the audience on all sides to just three.* FRANK *continues to dance as the music shifts from romantic to high-energy electronic music.* ANDREW *joins him for a moment as they do the Fist Bump together. They roll over to where there were previously audience seats and part the curtain that was hidden behind them.* KEN *is magically revealed, in a spotlight, out of his chair and sitting on a platform about a foot off the ground with his back to us, his chair parked beside the platform.* FRANK *and* ANDREW *move to the two doorways at the periphery of the performance space.*

> KEN *speaks into a glamorous makeup mirror at a vanity table. A camera projects a livestream video of his face, so we see both this close-up image and his reflection in the mirror.*

KEN: Jason.

I met Jason on the corner of Church and Alexander.
And I knew in the back of my mind,
Don't talk to him.
He's trouble.
But, do I listen?
No.
He has big hands and big feet.
So, I start to talk to him and I say,
"If I give you a hundred dollars, how would you like to come over for the night so I could massage and play with your feet?"

He says, "Okay."

So, we head back to my apartment.
As soon as we're in the apartment and the door's closed, I pay him a hundred dollars.
But then he turns it on me and says,
"How would you like to take a shower together?"
That wasn't part of our deal.
But, "Okay, fine."

So, I hop out of my chair,
take off my top
and pants
and socks,
but I leave on my underwear,
and bum into the bathroom.

> KEN *climbs down from the platform and bums across the floor, using his arms to move his seated torso.*

As soon as I'm in the bathroom,
he closes the door on me.
What the fuck's going on here?
What is he up to?
I try to open it, but I can't pull it.
What the fuck?
What's going on?
I pull it again,
I can't.

"HELP! HELP! HELP!"

And I try to open it again
and I can
a bit.
Enough that I'm able to put my hand through the door

and I feel something on the door handle.
I feel a rope.
And I'm thinking,
Where did that rope come from?
I didn't see it in his hand.
And somehow he tied the bathroom door to the apartment door.
I unhook it,
open up the door.
I bum out and he's nowhere to be found.
I look all over.
What the fuck!

    KEN *knocks on the floor.*

"Who is it?"

"The police."

Oh fuck, no.
"Come on in, it's open."

I'm still in my underwear.

And they come in
and I explain to them what happened.

And then I ask them,
"Are you going to charge him for locking me in my bathroom?"

"Only if we charge you."

"Me? Why?"

"You offered him money for sex."

Oh fuck.
I'm being screwed over,
first by Jason
and then by the cops.

And then they start to lecture me:
"You should be more careful who you invite in.
Because he could have hurt you
or killed you."

"Okay, fine."

After they leave, I'm thinking,
Aren't the police supposed to protect everybody in society?
Apparently not.
They would rather lecture Disabled people
than help and protect us.

And I'm still horny.

But do I learn?

Maybe . . .

> *As* KEN *bums back over to the platform,* FRANK *addresses* KEN *from his doorway position.*

FRANK: Just because we're disabled doesn't mean we should have to pay for sex.

KEN: Most guys in the community don't see me as a sexual being. Unless I pay for it. All they see is the chair.

FRANK: What do you mean, you think no one thinks you're sexy?

KEN: They don't. They don't see me as a sexual being. No one thinks I am.

Do you think I'm sexy? Do you?

> *FRANK watches as KEN hoists himself up on to the platform and into his chair.*

FRANK: When I first met you, your face was not the first I would have picked out from a crowd—

KEN: Bingo! Bingo!
And how long have you known me?

FRANK: Eight years.

KEN: And in that eight years did you ever see me as a sexual being?

FRANK: I'm doing my best to see you now, Ken.

KEN: I've been here in this community for over eighteen years, and even on Church Street I've been called "retarded" just because of how I look and how I talk. And it's taken you eight years to finally start to see me as a person, as a sexual person. Eight years!

> *KEN and FRANK are now at opposite doorways in the space. ANDREW moves into the centre, between them.*

ANDREW: Yeah, but just because we're disabled doesn't mean we can see each other either. I met a guy once who was in a chair. I met him online, noticed he was a wheelchair user, and I was really, *really* into that.

So, I invited him to my dorm room. I came downstairs to meet him, because I'm a classy cripple like that.

I remember he rolled in first, and I noticed we were at eye level. This was a new experience for me because, usually, when I'm with an able-bodied guy I have to do a lot of neck straining. But I didn't here. I was excited but nervous because, *How is this going to happen?* Somehow—I don't really know how—he managed to get us both into bed.

While we're having sex, I remember looking over and seeing the two empty chairs side-by-side and I thought, *Oh, isn't that cute! And hot!*

After, he left. I want to say I waited for three days, but really and truly I waited thirty minutes. I called and said:

> ANDREW *holds the phone to his ear.*

"Hey, man, thanks for . . . That was a really good time . . . uh . . . uh . . . Do you think maybe we could go for a movie or a coffee sometime?"

And he paused, and then he said, "Uh . . . yeah . . . about that, you were a bit too much work for me, I think you're too disabled."

> ANDREW *gasps in horror and glares at his phone. And then at us. And then at his phone. And then at us!*

He's not allowed to say that!!

> *As* ANDREW *moves to a corner doorway, the lights shift, isolating* FRANK *in a corner of the room.*

FRANK: I met Enrico the way I've met all the able-bodied guys in my life.

> *A soundscape of the pulsing beat of a dance floor at a gay bar.* FRANK *takes centre stage, grooving slightly to the music.*

I wanted to dance, so I went to the Barn. Crawled up three flights of stairs. Left my wheelchair downstairs. And I'm dancing on my knees, listening to the beat with my eyes closed.

I notice Enrico, and I look him up and down, up and down. He notices me checking him out. And he says, "What are you doing down there?"

"My wheelchair is parked downstairs."

"Stand on my feet!"

Okay . . . And he holds his hands out like this:

> FRANK *offers his hands, palms up.*

And I stand on his feet, and we dance.

> FRANK *sways, surrendering to the memory of* ENRICO's *embrace.*

And we're, like, pressed up close and it's sexy and it's hot and we close out the Barn. He helps me downstairs to my wheelchair. We walk—he walks and I wheel—all the way back to my apartment. But he doesn't come upstairs. First date.

> *The soundscape transitions to a distorted version of a 1980s power ballad as* FRANK *transitions to another memory.*

And then I'm at his apartment. And I'm lying on the bed and I can smell him. I'm listening to Air Supply's "Making Love Out of Nothing at All." He's at the inaccessible bathhouse *that I can't access* having sex with everyone, and I'm jealous.

> *The soundscape transitions to the beeping sound of a heart monitor in the hospital.*

And then we're at the Wellesley Hospital. And as we kiss, the hospital bed creaks. And he says, "I didn't see you when I was healthy. Not like *that*."

"Better late than never, Enrico."

And as we continue to kiss, he says, "I don't want you to catch my thrush."

"Honey, my immune system's fine and I'd have to drink litres of your saliva to catch the virus."

And we kiss again, and he says, "Out of all my lovers, no one else allows me to be sick. No one else allows me to be."

Enrico Franchella
breaking every rule.
Always shape shifting
changing.
Not fitting a mold.
Loved for his courage,
strength,
his ability to see others
and not through others.

New journeys and new beginnings
are never ending.
Remembering we are not here to see through each other.
We are here to see each other through.

> *Lights fade on* FRANK *as a projection draws our attention: the Scruff Chat window picking up where it left off. Lights slowly rise on* ANDREW *on his phone.*

> **BDC**
> So, we should hang out sometime, bro.

> **GB**
> Sure! Where you located?

You have just shared your location with Ginger Beef.

The location is the theatre!

> **GB**
> That's kinda far. But you're hot.

ANDREW: Okay!

> **BDC**
> So, is the wheelchair cool with you?

There is a pause.

> **GB**
> . . .
> Uh . . .

ANDREW: Ugh!

> **GB**
> Dunno.

ANDREW: Really?

> **GB**
> Maybe. I've never been with a disabled guy before.

ANDREW: Ahhh! so frustrating! I hate it when guys say that! Fucking dick.

ANDREW turns to the audience.

Could we all let out a scream of frustration? In whatever way you want to do it.

On the count of three, okay? One, two, three . . .

EVERYONE: Ahhh!

ANDREW: That was great! Thanks for that. That felt good. Hey, I have an idea. Can we get the house lights on?

The lights come up on the audience.

We can just turn this into a little game, okay? Hey, Ken, do you have anything you want to scream about?

KEN: People who steal off of me.

ANDREW: Oh yeah!

(to audience) Are you ready? One. Two. Three.

EVERYONE: Ahhhhh!

KEN: Hey Frank, do you have one?

FRANK: Yeah! Inaccessible dance clubs!

ANDREW: One! Two! Three!

EVERYONE: Ahhhhhhh!

ANDREW: That was fun. I think we can turn this into even more of a game. So, you know what? I'm going to take this side of the room—

He indicates a portion of the audience.

—from you to you right there.

KEN: And I'll take over here. From you until you.

FRANK: I guess that leaves me with this nice warm middle section.

> KEN, FRANK, *and* ANDREW *each talk to their group of audience members, inviting them to name their frustrations. In one performance, audience members suggested: "Donald Trump," "Guys who ghost me," "People who think that trans people aren't datable," or "The mold in my house." Guided by* KEN, FRANK, *and* ANDREW, *each group chooses their favourite frustration from among all the ideas brought forward by the group and presents it to the entire audience. The audience yells again for each group's chosen frustration. As the yell subsides . . .*

I've got a good one! A humongous one!
Trying to hide your boner at the Mormon Tabernacle!

> *Even if the audience yells with* FRANK, KEN *and* ANDREW *flee the performance space.*

KEN & ANDREW: Uh, I think that's just you, Frank! That's on you!

> FRANK, *now alone, takes centre stage. The house lights fade and the stage lights come up on* FRANK.

FRANK: I go to a gay Mormon conference in Salt Lake City and I'm standing in the line waiting to register.

> FRANK *positions himself as if he were waiting in a lineup.*

I'm in the first line and the second line is just over there.

> FRANK *indicates to his right.*

This really tall guy leans in and whispers—not whispers, he does it more like this: *(deep smoky voice)* "What's your fantasy?"

And I'm thinking, *My name's Frank but, okay, I can do this, I can play it your way.*

    FRANK *responds, imitating the tall guy's deep, smoky voice.*

"My fantasy is to have a very hot guy take me to see the Mormon Tabernacle Choir and to put his arm around me.

You know, just like all the other straight couples do in the Tabernacle."

That's a really boring fantasy. I mean he's probably not even going to respond to that.

    FRANK *rolls forward a little bit.*

The line moves up, and then he leans in to me and says, "My name's Travis."

"My name's Frank."

He says, "Who holds the door open for whom?"

"You're the tall one, you hold the door open for me."

So, Sunday arrives. We make our way to the Tabernacle. I roll into the accessible spot next to Travis.

    FRANK *wheels over to an audience member.*

(to audience member) Hi. It's nice to meet you.

    The audience member replies.

104 | INTERDEPENDENT MAGIC

Would you like to be my Travis?

> *They agree.* FRANK *rolls right in, closer beside them. He waits, expectant. Nothing happens.*

(whispering to the audience member) You have to put your arm around me!

> *They do.* FRANK *blushes, stealing sideways glances at his* TRAVIS.

We are listening to the prelude music, waiting for the choir to sing. He is very handsome, he makes me very nervous, and I bet he's a good kisser. And then the usher approaches and says, "What are you two gentlemen doing?"

"The same thing all the other couples are doing in the Tabernacle."

Travis leans in and he whispers, "Do you want to go home with me?"

> FRANK *looks to his* TRAVIS, *who may or may not play along and say the line as* TRAVIS.

"Yes! Yes, yes, yes, praise Jesus!"

> FRANK *thanks his* TRAVIS *and rolls to the centre of the space.*

And then, we get to the parking lot. At that time, I was driving a scooter, not a power chair. He puts the scooter in the back of the truck and we drive to Provo.

And then we are in his living room.

Sitting next to each other. We start to kiss—

> FRANK *closes his eyes, immersed in the memory.*

—and he puts his hand down, down to my loins.

> FRANK *startles, an involuntary movement. He is in distress.*

I open my eyes, he opens his eyes. His eyes soften and he says, "Did they shock you down there too?"

> FRANK *nods.*

And we start kissing again.

I get aroused again.

And this time I come.

> FRANK *does and his body freezes: back arched, limbs contracted, jaw clenched.*

And I'm spasming because I have cerebral palsy, and I open my eyes.

"Are you okay?"

"Ah, Travis, this is normal. It feels kind of good, but I don't normally let people see me come. It's too embarrassing. Could you just hold me for a little bit? It will subside. I just need time to let my body relax. It will be okay."

> *His body gently softens.*

And then he's holding me, and he's massaging me a bit, and we start kissing again and I'm relaxing. And then I open my eyes and look around at the living room and I see pictures of his wife. And his children.

> FRANK *leaves the memory.*

Travis wasn't going to be my eternal husband. We weren't going to be married in the Temple for time and all eternity. This was not going to be a happy-ever-after. But he was a stepping stone to healthy sex. To reaching a point in my life, in this moment, where the happiness and the love in my life is not codependent on anyone or anything. It just is.

I still believe in love. I still believe in romance. I still believe in magic!

> FRANK *pirouettes. Lush, romantic music plays as the lights shift.* KEN *appears in a suit and tie.*
>
> FRANK *reaches out his hand, beckoning to* KEN. KEN *closes the distance and embraces* FRANK.
>
> *They dance a dream ballet. They swirl around each other, hand in hand. They turn to face the audience and, as one, they lunge toward us and stop short,* FRANK *now standing in front of his chair.* FRANK *sits and* KEN *orbits around him,* FRANK *admiring* KEN's *grace.* KEN *stops directly in front of* FRANK, *who stands, steadying himself on* KEN's *chair, and nuzzles* KEN's *neck.* FRANK *sits and* KEN *sneaks up behind him, places his hands on* FRANK's *back and* FRANK *releases into* KEN's *embrace.* KEN *caresses* FRANK's *back as* FRANK *moves forward and away from* KEN, *but then he turns to face him. Holding hands, they circle, staring deep into each other's eyes. Finally, they land, face to face. They lean toward each other and embrace. It's intimate and sexy, romantic and dreamlike.*
>
> *As it ends,* FRANK *moves away and a video of* KEN *rolling along Toronto's waterfront path is projected, as the audio of the following monologue plays.* KEN *stays on stage, watching with us.*

KEN: *(voice-over)* Over the past year and a half,
I've gone from a gay
horny guy
who didn't care,
and now to a point
I do.
Even though I am still horny—
holy fuck am I ever.

I'm in a new home and a new part of town.
There are a lot of cute guys around,
and now it's summer
and sandals and bare feet,
And I'm starting to know some guys,
but it's been so hard,
and I don't know why.
Partly I do,
it's so hard not to want to ask them over.
But I've got a new place
and I want to protect it
and myself
more than I did before.

Before,
I would ask hustlers or homeless guys,
"Would you like to come over?
Do you need a place to stay?"
But now I'm working with escorts,
and they have their own places
and aren't drug addicts
or alcoholics.
Before I really didn't care,
even though I knew in the back of my mind,
that I most likely would end up burnt,
or hurt.
But now I'm asking more questions and setting boundaries.
I'm thinking with *this* head
instead of *this* head.

But I've still got the urge,
holy fuck, do I—

The film ends. KEN *turns to the audience.*

(live) It's hard not to ask, "Have you ever had a foot massage?"

The Scruff Chat window is projected on the wall, picking up where we left off.

GB
Maybe. I've never been with a disabled guy before.

BDC
Can I be your first?

GB
What can you do?

BDC
Come find out, Stud.

GB
I'll give it a try.

BDC
Great—come on over and I'll buzz you in.

GB
Cool. I'll be right there.

A buzz and a lighting change. At the rear of the performance space, curtains part to reveal a fully realistic yet stylized re-creation of ANDREW's *bedroom at home in pink, complete with bed, Hoyer lift (to transfer him from his chair to his bed), and* Phantom of the Opera *poster. He is looking hot, dressed for a date, in his wheelchair next to his bed. As he talks out loud to an imaginary Ginger Beef, his internal thoughts are expressed by a voice-over reviewing the situation.*

ANDREW: Hey.

(voice-over) Oh my God, he's actually here. Be cool. Take a breath. It'll be okay, it'll be fine. I mean it'll be great, right? Like, he's not a creep, right?

Come in.

Who is this guy? I mean, will he know what to do? Will he know how to take my pants off? What if I smell bad?

I'm glad you came over.

He doesn't want to be here—he probably feels obligated and then he'll resent me. What if I come too fast?

Can I get you anything?

That's so silly! I can't get him anything—he'll have to get it himself 'cause I'm disabled.

Make yourself comfortable.

Oh no—what if I have an IBS attack; what if I shit myself right now? What if I have to pee? He can't do a cath. What if I can't come? Then he'll never come back, and we won't move in together and have nights bingeing Netflix, and we'll never choose the china pattern for the gift registry for our accessible kitchen, and get the house with the white picket fence, and a Hoyer lift in every room, and a fleet of accessible vans, and adopt our four kids—Thomas, Christina, Don, and Riley, the little scamp—and we won't sit on the veranda watching our grandkids frolicking in the mist of the water sprinkler. Disability whyyyyy?!

DISABILITY WHYYYYYYY?!

    ANDREW *exits his room, moving quickly toward the audience.*

Why do I keep doing this?

Still, I'm here, and I kind of want to try.

(addressing audience) Tonight you've seen that we've cast some people in very special roles. I'm wondering if anybody from our very sexy audience would like to play my Ginger Beef tonight?

> ANDREW *surveys the audience.*

Anyone?

> *When a volunteer steps forward...*

Awesome! Can I ask you to come up here? There's something for you in my bag.

> *As they look into the bag hanging off the back of his chair, they find a ginger wig.*

Put it on.

> *Sometimes they're confused, thinking* ANDREW *wants to wear the wig.*

Put it on YOU.

> *The audience member puts it on.*

That looks amazing! You are now Ginger Beef.

> *This often earns them a round of applause.*

I'm wondering, can I ask you to come with me into my bedroom? If you feel comfortable ...

> *They agree.* ANDREW *and* GINGER BEEF *turn toward the bedroom and casually stroll on in.*

So, how are you doing? What have you been up to tonight?

> *They answer.*

At a show?

They usually say yes. They arrive in ANDREW's *bedroom. He gives them a tour of sorts.*

So, these are my stuffed animals, here's my *Phantom of the Opera* poster, and this is my Hoyer lift. Also, my friend is here—

He indicates the attendant that the audience met at the beginning of the show.

—as my "friend-tendant" if we need them.

Awkward hellos between GINGER BEEF *and the "friend-tendant."*

Would you like to hold my hand?

They agree.

I'm wondering if you would like to take off my shirt?

They say yes.

What you are going to do is lean me forward a little bit, and you're going to pull the shirt up over my head. Take my shoulders, and pull.

This takes a while. GINGER BEEF *is usually a bit tentative, but* ANDREW *is patient and affirming.*

You're doing great . . . Nearly there . . . Pull harder!

The shirt is off.

Okay, great. Now, know what I want you to do? I want you to throw it across the room like were going to make out. Passionately!

They throw the shirt.

I mean . . . Could you do that one more time? It wasn't quite passionate enough. Just like, like, throw it across the room *really* passionately. Okay go!

> *They retrieve the shirt and throw it again. Passionately!*

YESSS! So, these are my tattoos. Would you like to remove your shirt too? Maybe take it off passionately.

> *They rip off their shirt with reckless abandon and toss it aside. Or sometimes they don't.*

Would you like to get into bed with me?

> *They say yes.*

Okay. We're going to use this special machine. And I'm going to show you what to do.

> *ANDREW has pre-set his sling on his torso. He directs GINGER BEEF to retrieve the sling straps from under his thighs and behind his shoulders. He directs GINGER BEEF to attach the sling straps to the Hoyer lift. This takes quite a while. It is intimate, awkward, funny, and tender. And hot. Once the straps are safely secured to the lift . . .*

Okay, you're going to take the control thing from my "friend-tendant" there and you're going to press "up" all the way.

GINGER BEEF: All the way?

ANDREW: All the way.

> *ANDREW rises in the Hoyer lift. Slowly. Very slowly. He looks at the audience.*

Hey, everybody!

Once he is completely in the air . . .

Okay, this part of the show is private.

The curtain closes on ANDREW *and* GINGER BEEF. *Music begins to play: a karaoke version of "Short Dick Man" by 20 Fingers featuring Gillette. The space begins a transformation into a dance club.*

FRANK: HELLO, *(location of venue)*! Make some noise! I'm Frank, a.k.a. DJ Romance!

FRANK begins to sing an altered version of the song.

"Don't want no small foot man.
Don't want no small foot man.
Eeenie weenie little teeny, tiny little small foot man."

And, introducing Toronto's number one foot masseur, Ken! "Don't want no small foot man . . ."

FRANK continues singing as KEN *describes his ideal lover, listing their qualities, with* FRANK *sometimes improvising lyrics to support* KEN's *vision.*

KEN: My guy has to be at least six feet tall.
Big and wide feet.
Hairy all over.
Must be a heavy sleeper!

FRANK: *(speaking)* What in the world is that fucking thing? That has got to be the smallest little foot I have ever seen in my whole life!

KEN: He must have his own money.
His own place, his own job.
Must not be a drug addict or an alcoholic.

FRANK: *(backing up KEN)* I want a healthy relationship!

KEN: Must be patient.
Good in the kitchen and in bed.

FRANK: *(speaking)* What in the world is that smelly thing? That has got to be the smelliest foot I have ever smelled in my whole life. Get the fuck over here.

KEN: He must love foot massages.
Must love and respect me and not take advantage of me because I'm in a chair.
And must not mind that I cannot fuck him.

FRANK: *(to KEN)* I guess that means he fucks you.

KEN: Yeah!

FRANK: And now, let's give a cheer for your Number One Queer Cripple. Your Disabled Dork With A Big Dick: ANDREW!

> *The curtains part. ANDREW emerges from his room in a leather harness and leather cap. The three performers dance some slick choreography together.*

ANDREW: And introducing: Ginger Beef!

> *The volunteer audience member emerges, wearing a "Disabled People Are Hot" T-shirt. KEN, FRANK and ANDREW lead the audience in applause for GINGER BEEF. They all turn to the audience.*

The show is over, people, but let's get this party started!

KEN: Hit it, DJ!

FRANK: Get ready to access me.

ANDREW: And me!

KEN: And me!

> *The performance space has completed its transition from a bare performance space in the round into a fully accessible dance club. A bar is revealed, tables of snacks magically materialize, blacklight images of stylized sexy wheelchairs appear on the walls.*
>
> *Everyone is free to enjoy themselves.*

ACCESS ME APPENDIX

Question Cards

What are you into?
How do you identify?
What turns you on?
If I date you, will I have to be your attendant?
Do you prefer to have sex in your chair or in a bed?
How often do you masturbate?
Are you proud to be gay and disabled?
How do I flirt with you?
What's your type?
Do you wish you could walk?
Should I come to your level when I talk to you?
Is it cool to offer you help?
Do you have any kinks or fetishes we can explore together?
How do you meet guys?
How do you have sex?
Is it okay to ask about your disability?
How do you go to the bathroom?
How do you get in and out of your chair?
What do you wish you could experience in bed?

NEURODIVERGENCE AND INTERDEPENDENT PRACTICE: A CONVERSATION WITH NIALL MCNEIL BY BECKY GOLD

The work of neurodivergent artists within Canada's Disability performance ecology is vastly under-represented in contrast to the work of artists with physical or sensory disabilities. While there are a number of companies and collectives (past and present) that have focused on training and performance opportunities for this community, these artists often go unacknowledged within the wider Disability arts sector, as well as within the culture of theatre and performance in Canada more broadly. With that, I echo the sentiment of Disability arts scholar Tony McCaffrey, who suggests that theatre by neurodivergent artists is "a theatre whose time has come."[1]

While there are a number of companies that have been working with neurodivergent artists for decades, a notable shift in perspective and practice has been emerging. The role of the non-disabled director "giving a voice to" neurodivergent artists has begun to diminish and, in turn, neurodivergent minds and voices are coming to the fore as leaders, creating theatre that serves their own unique interests and ways of working.

To date, the greatest example of the pursuit of this exciting shift in collaborative creation by neurodivergent artists in Canada is the work of Niall McNeil. Niall is a Vancouver-based artist with Down syndrome best known for his work as co-writer and performer in Neworld Theatre's *King Arthur's Night*, which premiered in 2017 at Toronto's Luminato Festival

---

1   McCaffrey, Tony. *Incapacity and Theatricality: Politics and Aesthetics in Theatre Involving Actors with Intellectual Disabilities.* Routledge, 2019.

before moving on to a run at the National Arts Centre. The show was then remounted in 2018 at Vancouver's PuSh festival and in 2019, travelled abroad for a brief run at the No Limits Festival in Hong Kong.

Niall has been a tour de force in pushing the boundaries of Disability arts leadership and he continues to pave the way showing how artistic roles can be reframed and reimagined within the context of interabled[2] collaboration.

Niall's primary collaborator has been Siminovitch Prize–winning playwright Marcus Youssef. Together, Niall and Marcus have developed a method of collaboration that both privileges and celebrates Niall's unique world view and poetic writing style within their joint story and script development. Years prior to *King Arthur's Night*, Niall and Marcus collaborated on a co-production between Vancouver's Leaky Heaven Circus and Neworld Theatre titled *Peter Panties*. This production, which premiered in 2011, was a reimagining of the story of Peter Pan through Niall's eyes—incorporating elements of Shakespeare's *Macbeth* as well as characters from the early 2000s TV series *CSI*.

The scripts for both *Peter Panties* and *King Arthur's Night* were published as a small collection by Talonbooks in 2018.

While Niall has gained recognition in the last few years as a truly valuable contributor to Canada's Disability performance scene, he is in fact a veteran artist. Niall has been performing since the age of five and developed his love for theatre during his summers spent at Caravan Farm Theatre in Armstrong, British Columbia. Niall talks about his experience at the Caravan with deep fondness and nostalgia, reminiscing not only about his time performing there, but also about doing farm work and spending time with friends.

I first had the pleasure of formally meeting Niall (and his mom, Joan) in June 2017 at the National Art Centre's Deaf, disability and Mad arts summit and Republic of Inclusion. This time was particularly busy for Niall as he was in tech rehearsals for the run of *King Arthur's Night* at the NAC. However, we stayed in touch as I expressed interest in working with

---

2   I use to the term "interabled" to refer to relationships between those who have lived experience of disability and those who do not. The term interabled is commonly used to describe romantic relationships between a disabled and non-disabled individual, though that is not my intention here.

him. That fall, I was hired to be Niall's "creative assistant"—this essentially meant that I would be working with him as a support worker for any upcoming creative projects. Our first creative endeavour was attending a multi-week playwriting workshop at Playwrights Theatre Centre (PTC) in Vancouver. Niall was the only disabled participant in the cohort, and so we worked together to navigate the workshops in ways that best suited him and his learning and writing style.

Together we began developing a script for Niall's adaptation of *Beauty and the Beast*—a project that he is still working on. We created hand-drawn storyboards to outline the play and I would transcribe on my laptop as Niall, with such confidence and fluidity of thought, would recite dialogue between multiple characters. He had all of the scenes figured out in his mind, and it was my job to simply get them down on the page. Our experience together at PTC was in many ways challenging, but we found a method of collaboration and script development that worked for us. After the workshop concluded, Niall and I continued working and writing together until I left Vancouver in the summer of 2018 to pursue my PH.D. in Toronto. My experience of working with Niall was always joyful and full of laughter. I found myself drawn to his particular use of language and imaginative description in his writing. As noted so eloquently by one of Niall's other collaborators, Anton Lipovetsky, "he writes in a gorgeously specific and poetic idiom,"[3] and I could not agree more.

As I am now based in Toronto and Niall is still living and working in Vancouver, we don't get to see each other as much as we used to. However, I always make a point of paying him a visit when I'm back in town.

When asked by Jessica if I would be interested in interviewing Niall for this anthology, I jumped at the opportunity. I was excited to once again work collaboratively with Niall and for him to be able to speak for himself about his work, to highlight his methods as a practitioner, and to be able to capture his passion for the performing arts in his own words.

The interview that follows is an amalgamation of two fairly casual one-hour Zoom interviews that took place in July 2020. It is divided into

---

3   Bakogeorge, Alethea. "Meet Anton Lipovetsky, Our New Crescendo Artist." Musical Stage Company, 2020. https://musicalstagecompany.com/meet-anton-lipovetsky-our-new-crescendo-artist/.

six sections: Introduction, Writing Process, Project Inspiration, Access and Support, Upcoming Projects, and Final Thoughts.

INTRODUCTION

BECKY: All right, Ni, well, we're just going to get started. How about you just introduce yourself to me and pretend that I don't know you at all. Tell me a little bit about yourself . . .

NIALL: *(laughter)* You know me!

BECKY: I do!

NIALL: Oh, I see. When I first met you . . .

BECKY: Yeah, if you just met me for the first time, how would you introduce yourself to me?

NIALL: Okay. My name is Niall Patrick McNeil. I am a . . . a nice guy. I am a song-lyric writer, actor, and a poet . . . slowly learning to be a director. I have two Jessie Awards from *Peter Panties* and *King Arthur's Night*.

BECKY: Can you tell me about how you first got started in theatre? Do you remember what your first show was?

NIALL: I was in the Caravan [Farm Theatre] . . . but when I first started theatre, I think was when I came out of Mom's stomach. [I have been going to the Caravan] since I was five. My first show was *As You Like It*. That's the first show I was ever in. And after that it was *Bull by the Horns*, *Romeo and Juliet*; it was *Strange Medicine*, [and] *Beggar's Opera*.

BECKY: Do you remember what it was like when you did your very first play? How you felt about it?

NIALL: When I first be on stage, I feel a bit scared. But I don't need to be scared. There's some other actors on stage to comfort me and I think it was a great opportunity.

WRITING PROCESS

BECKY: And you're a two-time published playwright now!

NIALL: I write song lyrics mostly. The lyrics I do with Veda Hille. She's a composer. She can play on her keyboard or guitar or her bass.

BECKY: How do you write with Veda?

NIALL: Well, I give some lyrics to Veda. I translate my words into my phone and send it to Veda, and she can change it any time she wants.

BECKY: So, that's how you collaborate on your song lyrics?

NIALL: We're collaborators.

BECKY: When you're sending the lyrics, do you send just the words, or do you sing it?

NIALL: I can sing it if I have a wild imagination.

BECKY: What's your favourite part about writing songs?

NIALL: You have to be patient. You have to be patient with dictation.

BECKY: Yeah, dictation software can be challenging sometimes, eh?

NIALL: I like to write it, but the dictation says that I said "washing hands" and I don't mean to say that, and I get frustrated so I delete the words [and type them out manually] . . . "walk to the hallways and meet each other again." It takes time to say what you want to say to dictation.

BECKY: Can you tell me a bit about what it's like when you're writing a script? You've written a few plays now with Marcus [Youssef].

NIALL: Same thing. Our cellphones. Sometimes when he's here [at my house], he sits down, and he types on his computer and he records everything. My words, *not* his words.

BECKY: Do you have a favourite part about writing?

NIALL: Me and Marcus like to make jokes before we start. The writing part is kind of not really my favourite, but it's like . . . I'd say my favourite part is to be one of the actors and read a script, doing tech, or that kind of stuff.

BECKY: What are your goals as a playwright?

NIALL: Keep writing until I'm sixty-five. Sixty-five or sixty-six. Keep writing until I'm tired.

PROJECT INSPIRATION

BECKY: Ni, I'm curious about how you come up with ideas for your plays. Let's start with *Peter Panties*. Can you tell me what made you interested in Peter Pan as a character?

NIALL: It's because I want to write my own play people can see. Peter Pan who didn't want to be a man . . . he just wants [to be a] little boy . . . have fun.

BECKY: And did you feel like that when you were interested in writing about Peter Pan?

NIALL: Yeah!

BECKY: You just wanted to have fun?

NIALL: Yeah.

BECKY: Yeah, I get that. Okay, same kind of question for your other play—can you tell me about why you were interested in writing about King Arthur?

NIALL: He's the lead guy; somebody had to do it.

BECKY: So, he was a leader?

NIALL: He's a star. He has knights. He can do jokes too.

BECKY: Well, you did jokes in your version, right?

NIALL: Yeah.

BECKY: Do you think the original King Arthur was funny or do you think he was serious?

NIALL: No, not. Sometimes he is serious. Sometimes he gets angry and calls his guards.

BECKY: Do you have a favourite scene in *King Arthur*?

NIALL: I like the scene with Tiffany and I dancing—"Two Wars."

BECKY: Do you have a favourite song?

NIALL: "Seven Things About Guinevere."

BECKY: You mentioned Tiffany. What was it like for you to work on *King Arthur* with other performers with Down syndrome?

NIALL: Me and Andrew [Gordon] are athletes. I've probably known him since floor hockey. Matthew [Tom-Wing] . . . I didn't know him at first. Where we first met . . . we did a workshop at DSRF [Down

Syndrome Research Foundation]. We did a warmup, have fun and play some music and make some scenes together. The Down Syndrome Research Foundation. That's where I first met them. I was clocking Tiff [King], Matthew, and Andrew. Incredible, they're all so incredible that I worked with.

ACCESS AND SUPPORT

BECKY: Let's talk a bit about support. When other people are working with you, what is helpful for them to know about the ways that you work? What makes things easier for access?

NIALL: Access needs. For my access needs . . . I get tired really easy, worn down, and I get sad emotion. That's kind of the access needs I have.

BECKY: What about talking fast? If somebody's talking very quickly?

NIALL: [If someone] is speaking really fast and I can't understand what they're saying, it's a bit challenging.

BECKY: So, what do you say when somebody's talking too fast with you?

NIALL: Slow down with me, please.

BECKY: Yeah, and you're pretty good about letting people know when they're talking too fast.

NIALL: I try to.

BECKY: Yeah, I think that's really important.

NIALL: What do you mean by important?

BECKY: I think a lot of people don't realize that talking so fast means that you can't understand or other people with disabilities can't understand. So, I think it's really important and very brave of you when you say, you know, "Hey, I think you need to slow down." I think that's really good. Any other kinds of support that are helpful for you?

NIALL: I get a lot of support [listing off roster of support workers]. I went down to Commercial Drive, got coffee, but I don't need support for that.

BECKY: Yeah, you can do that by yourself. Anything else you want to share about access needs or support for you as an artist?

NIALL: As an artist, you do need to have support to create a new thing.

UPCOMING PROJECTS

BECKY: You have some exciting projects coming up like *Cowboy Tempest*. Can you tell me about why you wanted to write a version of *The Tempest* about cowboys?

NIALL: I think it all began when me and Lucy [McNulty] were in the farm truck talking about what is *The Tempest*. I was at the Caravan ... some people can act like being cowboys. Outlaws that ride on a horse, they're driving wagons and they're always getting into fights.

BECKY: Right, so you were inspired by the Caravan? That farm life?

NIALL: Yeah, farm life, country life.

BECKY: So, it's kind of like *The Tempest*, but a western?

NIALL: Yeah. It's mainly about Prospero doing all kinds of magic ... It's mainly about him raising his daughter ... it's really complicated because my version [is like a] cabaret kind of. Prospero, Sebastian ... that's just regular *Tempest,* but we're using that for the plot, and then we shape the plot. So, Prospero had a daughter and they were both stranded in a hot, hot desert for ... stranded for twelve years.

And Antonio's in the country, that's Prospero's brother. He wants to get revenge on him. Prospero came walking to the twenty-four-hour diner to meet Amber, because Amber is Prospero's wife . . . there's a diner in the middle of nowhere. There's coffee, eggs, whatever they want to cook, and there's a guy named Caliban trying to spit into the food, put alcohol in the food, explosion with coffee everywhere.

BECKY: So, does Caliban work at the diner?

NIALL: Yeah, he was.

BECKY: Okay.

NIALL: Spit.

BECKY: Oh no . . .

NIALL: Clipping his fingernails in it . . . That's what he does. He can't help it. And so, Miranda says, "Don't do it, or else I'll have to tell my dad about it!" So, it's kind of like that . . . That's so far what I have in my brain.

FINAL THOUGHTS

BECKY: What are five things that you would like people to know about you?

NIALL: One, they can search my name on the computer. You can type in my name . . . There's some links on YouTube. Two, learn about Down syndrome. Three, don't talk too quickly. Four is bear with me, because I'm a slow talker, and the fifth one is if I have editing software, I might be slow.

BECKY: What does that mean?

NIALL: It means when I'm reading and highlighting, it takes me time to delete some words or put some words in.

BECKY: Okay, so your editing process is a little bit slower and people will need to be patient?

NIALL: Yep.

BECKY: Awesome! Anything else you want to say before we go?

NIALL: I think... I loved to chat with you during the interview. I like to share my work with you. That's it.

BECKY: Awesome! Well, it was great to see you, Ni.

NIALL: Okay, Becky. Let's talk again soon.

BECKY: Absolutely! We'll talk again soon Ni.

NIALL: Say hi to Alex [Bulmer].

BECKY: I will! Bye, Ni!

ANTARCTICA
BY SYRUS MARCUS WARE

INTRODUCTION
BY YOUSEF KADOURA

I first got to know Syrus the summer after I graduated from the National Theatre School of Canada, at the Republic of Inclusion in Ottawa. It had brought together Mad, Deaf, and Disabled artists from across Canada and the UK for two weeks to create together and discuss Disability and Accessibility in the arts. On the last day I was loitering outside the stage door when Syrus stopped for a chat. He had been one of the coordinators of the event, and we had grown close over those last two weeks. He was wondering where I was going next now that I had left Montreal. I knew I was in a travelling mood, but I wasn't sure where I wanted to go. The Republic, however, helped me realize that what I had been wanting was to take part in the community, and Syrus confirmed it by telling me about the Crip community in Toronto. Sure, I've since discovered that Toronto is way too expensive, poorly designed, and in dire need of better social services and more bike lanes; but the people and the community are far too kind and compelling for me to consider being anywhere else at this moment in time.

After a couple of years of being in the city, taking on as many different roles and experiences as I could manage, Syrus called and asked me to meet with him and a few other artists at a bar in Kensington Market. It was there I was introduced to Dainty Smith and Ravyn Wngz, the two powerhouse performers with whom I was eventually going to journey through a performative exercise unlike any I had done before. It was *Antarctica*, the show Syrus was recruiting us for. As an activist, Syrus is intensely aware of injustice and the state of the globe, and in his readings he'd come across the Antarctic Treaty. Prompted by the Cold War, this treaty is a colonialist pact created in 1959 between twelve nations that divvies up the continent between them in case of global nuclear annihilation. In Syrus's *Antarctica* it is climate change and not nuclear fallout that triggers the treaty; the complete failure to protect the earth leads to Antarctica being on the way to becoming one of the last habitable land masses on the planet. It is, I would argue, not too dissimilar a path to the one we are currently on, unfortunately. In response to the crisis in Syrus's *Antarctica*, the treaty nations have sent citizens to stake their claims on borders by giving birth to children. The parallels to what is happening now in our world, both on a global scale and in Antarctica specifically, are disconcerting, and it is something we need to be paying attention to.

Syrus wanted to bring this to people's attention through the stage, and for the three of us to take on the roles of Antarcticans acting as envoys from their imagined nations to the wide white continent. They would make up a wealth of identities—Trans, Queer, Disabled, and BIPOC folk—these identities also being part of our real as well as imagined identities.

The play was first presented at the 2019 SummerWorks festival in Toronto, and then at the Toronto Biennial of Art, where it ran three times weekly for several months. The Biennial performance took place within an installation created by Syrus, transforming what was once a garage into the shelters inhabited by the Antarcticans. The shelters were represented on a set that was drained of colour, paramilitary-style shelves held a dwindling supply of rations and survival equipment, while the work and sleep areas were similarly utilitarian. The environment was created through hanging textiles and a video projection of the North. The installation not only gave us an imaginative playground to perform in, but also allowed us to create spaces representative of our characters. It invited the audience into the environment itself, where they could be physically transported to the same space where we as actors were suspending our disbelief. Syrus's creation was so effective I still have clear memories of shivering from the cold of Antarctica.

A key thing, which I think we all discovered as we moved through the piece, was just how much the play is shaped by the threat of white supremacy. Just as European colonization is an act of white supremacy, so is this colonization of Antarctica; it is the wealthy who take advantage of the destruction of the land through global warming. The first Antarcticans are diverse non-white individuals, and they are sent at the earliest and most dangerous stage to pave the way for the "rightful owners," their governing bodies in this case, who solely represent the interests of the ruling class.

This play can be horrifying when taken at face value. The difficulties humanity has experienced the last few centuries are being overshadowed by our current global crisis. The reality of global warming, epidemics, and the resurgence of fascism are just the beginning of the challenges we are collectively facing. Speculative fiction is becoming less fictitious the closer we look at it.

To draw from previous literatures, I would liken *Antarctica* to George Orwell's *1984* in that it gives us an opportunity to reflect and learn from our future before it happens. I cannot say that the knowledge held within this piece will save us from the future, just as *1984* certainly did not save us from the surveillance state. However, I do believe it gives Queer, Crip, and BIPOC folk a social roadmap for the future and fast approaching scientific realities. This play maintains the hope that we can still pursue a better life for all people and the generations who will follow. It does not give us permission to give up on the world by presenting a doomsday-like prophecy of things to come, but rather a dream for our collective futures.

Antarctica was first produced at the SummerWorks Performance Festival as part of the Lab Series in partnership with the Toronto Biennial of Art in August, 2019, at the Theatre Centre, Toronto, with the following cast and creative team:

Yousef Kadoura
Dainty Smith
Ravyn Wngz

Director: Syrus Marcus Ware
Design: Merlin Hargreaves and Syrus Marcus Ware

CHARACTERS

Sabian
Jessica
Marcus

SCENE ONE

November 19, 2025, Project Antarctica has begun. Eleven ships carrying the land-borns and their supplies have departed and will have set up the first Antarctic colonies by late 2047.

SABIAN: Log 278. November 2025.

How we fucking got here.

Okay, so . . .

The treaty planned for a Cold War moment; for the perceived threats of 1959.

The treaty says nothing about the changing climate.

The powerful in 1959 didn't predict the need for Antarctica, the need for the continent to be a livable space.

Now, in 2025, with its ice mostly melted, Antarctica is one of the few fertile land masses left on the earth.

The powerful left questions about the process of colonizing the continent.

Leaving us to figure this shit out for ourselves. Leaving our powerful to make the decisions about our lives.

She sighs.

This is stupid. Why am I still doing my daily logs? Because I'm hoping that somehow someone somewhere will hear these and know what happened to us? Hear the truth of what happened here?

Eleven of us had been born at that point on the Antarctic ice. One was born in the '70s, an accidental occurrence during a science expedition.

But all of the rest of us ten were sent there to be born, to stake a future land claim through birthright. We were born in Antarctic waters, our fates set for us from that moment forward.

Marcus?

SCENE TWO

JESSICA: Fifty, fifty-one, fifty-two, fifty-three. Fuck. I need to get the next shipment, like, yesterday. But the next one isn't due until . . .

Fuck. Six months. Six months if the fires don't burn down the food stores beforehand. If the government doesn't dissolve and leave us here alone.

No. No. The government will not disappoint us. They will send the rations. I'm supposed to trust in the plan.

I have to, right?

"We are the Antarcticans. We will find safety for the inhabitants of Earth. We will build a new world for our chosen few, make a new world together."

It's probably the tarps. AH!

SABIAN: AHHH!

JESSICA: Fuck, Sabian. What the fuck are you doing here?

Here to start a revolution?

SABIAN: Jessica. Still carrying heat I see.

JESSICA: What do you waaaant, Sabian? I'm busy. Actually planning for our survival here, instead of running around playing activist.

SABIAN: I am an activist. I'm not playing—let me make myself perfectly clear.

And I'm actively trying to make a better life for us. I want something better for us than . . . this?

Don't you?

Jessica, you can't tell me that after everything that's happened, the lack of communication, the lack of provisions and supplies, the sheer and utter lack of help from our home countries—you can't tell me that you are still pro-company after all of this?

JESSICA: Why does everything have to be a fight with you? These are the end times. We are LUCKY to be here. We are going to survive. If you can't see that, I can't help you.

SABIAN: But when is colonization okay? We've never even been to the centre of Antarctica—no one has. What if there are people living there? Or other, non-human animals. This shit ain't right.

JESSICA: Sabian . . . Have you eaten?

SABIAN: Can we talk about what happened?

JESSICA: Sabian—it happened. It's over. Let's just say we were in need of each other and fulfilled that need. I'm not here to find lovers. I'm here to save the world. I have my mission, you have yours.

SABIAN: We're going away.

JESSICA: What? Where? Who's we?

SABIAN: To Mary Byrd Land. Me and Marcus, when the spring comes.

JESSICA: To Mary Byrd Land!? No one has ever been there—it's far too treacherous to reach on land, and ships can't pass that way—and there's no infrastructure there and there's no life and—

SABIAN: Jess—we've got a plan. We leave in four months when the weather is warmer.

Come with us.

JESSICA: You're completely bananas! I'm not going anywhere! How could you even ask me that? I'm not risking my life to end up exactly where? On the wrong side of the continent cut off from everything—

Laughing in disbelief.

No way. No thank you.

SABIAN: *(crushed)* That's . . . what I thought you'd say, I guess. Well, think about it.

JESSICA: I've got to finish my counting.

BOTH: What was that?

SABIAN: Probably the tarps . . .

SCENE THREE

SABIAN: White supremacy is everywhere here—everything on this damn continent is white. I mean every fucking thing here . . . is . . . white. Are you telling me you're okay with this? This is what they want, an all-white Antarctica—a space where only they survive. Us being here is incidental.

MARCUS: I mean, on the one hand, of course not. How could I be okay with it all? I know the company is evil . . . but what choice do we have, really? It's not like we have money or people or any of the things we'd need to try to take over this land—we are two people!

What you're proposing could work—with maybe five hundred more people. Sabian—it's just us. We don't really have a choice here. At least if we go along, we'll be guaranteed a space in the end, too.

SABIAN: Listen to yourself! You're like an ad for neo-liberalism right now!

MARCUS: Sabian! Listen—

SABIAN: No, you listen! We wouldn't actually need to do much to fuck this shit up.

Think about it. All we have to do is shut off communication to the North—the rich will have no way of knowing what is happening down here.

And then we can take over, encampment by encampment, winning the others over to our cause. To the creation of a free Antarctica. Or at least freeing ourselves from . . . this?

We can do this. I have organized more with less. Okay, maybe not less.

MARCUS: It won't work.

SABIAN: Marcus!

MARCUS: It won't.

SABIAN: There's one other option though . . . I mean, it's a long shot. But I read about it before I came here. It's Mary Byrd Land. The unclaimed territory in the south of the island. Who says we need to spend any time tearing down what they want us to build. What if we sidestep that altogether and build our own new world from the ground up—in the free territory?

MARCUS: I can't believe I'm saying this, but . . . tell me more.

SABIAN: We could cut off communication with the North, as I was saying . . . but then just leave. Move to Mary Byrd Land and then start a new community, a free space where people can come to live if they can make it here. A space for us and our people.

MARCUS: How would we get there? That land is across four time zones! That means four borders and I'm not sure we'd ever get across four borders. FOUR borders? It's impossible.

SABIAN: We could go by water . . . around the shoreline.

MARCUS: We don't have accurate maps. The Pine Glacier has fallen away; it could be out there floating as smaller icebergs, ready to rip our ships in half.

SABIAN: We'll swim there. We can use our thermal regulators.

The regulators, they have a five-hour charge . . . so we will have to take breaks, but we'll need them to rest.

We could do this. We could.

MARCUS: *(whispers softly)* Well, fuck!

We could . . .

He trails off in awe.

Could our regulators work for that long? We're talking many days in the water.

I'm not sure I could swim for that long, I get tired . . .

SABIAN: So, we bring extra battery packs and float them with us while we swim. And we can take breaks on the ice flows . . .

We could do this, Love. We could.

We could leave. We could fucking free ourselves from this confinement.

Hey. So, I'm thinking . . . we can't leave Jessica here. I know shit is hella complicated right now, but I just couldn't leave her . . . here?

Gestures around.

I mean, anyways, BIPOCs gotta stick together, right? Especially in this place?

MARCUS: Ha! She's a company fan! We'll never get her to come, but go right ahead and try. I know you like wasting your time, energy, supplies . . .

SABIAN: Enough Marcus . . .

Anyways, you know I love a challenge.

But seriously. Are you telling me you'd be okay leaving her here . . . to snow, to whiteness, to the eventually overrunning of this place by rich people?

MARCUS: What if she says no, but then knows our plans? Like, think about it, though . . . Can we trust her to keep this secret?

SABIAN: What was that?

MARCUS: It's probably the tarps.

SCENE FOUR

MARCUS: Jess?

JESSICA: Marcus! What are you doing here? Do borders mean nothing to you people? And it's Jessica.

MARCUS: Ha! I've been spending too much time with Sabian. I guess they don't anymore.

JESSICA: So, why are you here? What are you protesting now?

MARCUS: Naw. I'm not one for protesting.

Do you know what I was doing before I was deployed here?

Absolutely nothing.

I mean nothing of importance. My life was just getting and securing food and water and not much else. Day in, day out.

When the company offered me a free trip to this icy paradise, of course I went for it.

Not that I had much of a choice.

Laughing.

I couldn't care less about the company, and I certainly don't want to waste my time protesting it.

I just wanna have what I need and be safe. Safer? You know what I mean.

JESSICA: Why did you come here?

MARCUS: Jess— Jessica—I came because I guess I wanted to convince you to come with us.

JESSICA: Marcus!

MARCUS: I wanted to convince you to come with us, because . . . well, we need you. I think Sabian and I will kill each other if we are left alone to our devices!

Laughing.

No, but really, Jess . . . ica. Come with us.

It's not gonna be safe here in the long run. Either we're gonna be successful and set up the colonies and the rich folks are gonna come and turf us, or we fail and we die here, alone, after our governments crumble.

Think about it—the crumbling . . . It's already happening. When was your last dispatch from home?

They're off schedule, right?

Laughs.

Mine are too.

JESSICA: Marcus. I'm staying. Let me finish my work. I've got my log still to do.

MARCUS: You're still doing your daily logs? Man, you are a company hero.

JESSICA: I'm doing what I was assigned to do. It's called working and I'm lucky to have a job to do in this world. In case you hadn't noticed, it's on fire and we are basically the last chance for humanity! Our governments have trusted us with this duty. I'm serving the best way I know how.

MARCUS: Jessica! You can't be this right-wing! Not after what the governments have done to us all. How they've fucked us globally with this climate change. How they waited until the last moment and then sent us here when it's probably already too late . . .

JESSICA: I'm not right-wing! I just believe in some things that you don't. Like in our homelands, in the people we have elected to run those homelands. In the will of the constituents. All of our citizens who are praying for us to be successful so that they will have a place to come to. If you can't see that as being important, we have nothing left to discuss.

MARCUS: What about Sabian?

JESSICA: Not important, Marcus. We have nothing left to discuss . . .

MARCUS: Why couldn't they have waited until this place had thoroughly thawed out?

JESSICA: We had to come here now . . .

Every fucking one said it was time. The Antarctic plan had to begin.

We had to come now. Don't you remember your training?

MARCUS: The fucking training! It was a joke. Fifty-four weeks in the arctic where the temperatures were twenty degrees Celsius and nothing like here. Learning skills I'll never need and missing the ones that would keep me alive here. A fucking joke!

I just did what I had to. I wanted to come here—I needed a secure place and somewhere to actually put down roots. I was glad to come here. It wasn't any patriotic shit.

JESSICA: Patriotism? I'm not talking about patriotism.

I'm talking about knowing where your next meal is coming from and staying true to that source.

You know, there was Antarctic tourism? Rich tourists by the boatloads. Can you believe people wasting their money on this crap while the world was on fire??

My government vowed to put a stop to it, by patrolling the waters more, by denying permits . . .

I voted for them and I believe in what they are trying to do.

MARCUS: Come with us, Jess. Sabian would—

JESSICA cuts him off.

JESSICA: Marcus! I'm so tired of this conversation.

She slumps mockingly.

MARCUS: You know they protested? Me coming here I mean. The ableist assholes in my home country didn't trust their lives—no, their livelihoods—to a disabled person. Didn't think I was up to the rigour of the job.

JESSICA: Fuck! Marcus.

MARCUS: No, Jessica, I want you to realize, people are assholes sometimes! You are so willing to do anything for your country, but would they do the same for you?

There's few real people out there, people who get justice and self-determination and the need for all of us to get to make it, not just the rich few.

Shit. I do sound like Sabian. And speaking of Sabian— She's one of the few people who really gets it, I mean—

MARCUS gets cut off.

JESSICA: Marcus! Enough already. It's time to go. And just so you know—they weren't exactly thrilled it was me *(gestures to skin)* coming here either. But I'm who they have and I'm here to do my duty. I've got work to do. Goodbye, Marcus!

MARCUS hesitates, then puts his hands up. Then leaves.

JESSICA starts back on her log.

"I remember when I had my first meeting with the company.

At my meeting, they told me to avoid eastern Antarctica, it was so much colder than the west due to its elevation. They told me that a one-room portable was being airlifted from my home to the east for my efforts. They told me to get settled in and begin to set up a life there—living and establishing roots were one of the ways of ensuring the land claim.

I was warned that the other eleven countries were also sending delegates— and that they would do everything they could to stake claim, to try to push the boundaries of the treaty—and to watch out for tricks or pitfalls.

Of course, I was nervous. New people, new places, leaving everything behind.

But I believe in the company. And honestly? I couldn't imagine more loneliness, more than my life at that time, and I was ready for something more to happen beyond trips to the rations station and the pressures of a life of isolation. I was going to have a fucking purpose."

They are nuts. They will never survive. It's a fool's mission. What will happen to their camps? What will happen to their territories? It's gonna be a massive land grab by someone. When it's discovered that they are gone, that is. That could take months.

Months . . .

Okay. "We reached the Antarctic waters on November 20, 2045 . . . "

SCENE FIVE

SABIAN: How did you know it was the end of the world? At what point did you realize we were fucked?

MARCUS: I guess I never really knew, not for sure. Like, is this fire the end? Is that one? Is this government dissolution a sign of the end or just part of the same old? I was never really sure. Not until just before they started the Mars mission.

SABIAN laughs excitedly.

SABIAN: That fucking Mars mission! A thousand of the world's richest on a one-way ticket to paradise, except with the wrong calculations even ships of the rich can become doomed. Imagine: all those people, doomed.

MARCUS: I never thought I'd hear you be sympathetic about a bunch of rich people dying.

SABIAN: It's complicated—I had a terrible relationship with my family, but I still didn't want them to go on that ship. Now we will never have a chance to resolve our shit.

MARCUS: Wait, your family is on that ship. You all were . . . rich?

SABIAN: I wasn't! But, yeah, my parents were, and I benefited from that access.

MARCUS: Shit! I guess it's true what they say—we don't talk about class enough in our organizing.

MARCUS laughs.

What did your activist friends think about that? The great Sabian, a rich kid whose family took the first ship out of here when shit got real.

SABIAN: I know my family is fucked but, like, don't talk about them, okay—you don't know the situation. We'd been estranged for years, since my first arrest for activism. And I wasn't exactly invited along on their trip to paradise—not that I would have gone.

MARCUS: Shit. Sorry, Sabian, you're right. They left you here, and before this mission. Anyways, it's just surprising—people always got down on me for not being more involved, but I was working to eat and live . . . If I'd had your cushioning . . . who knows what I'd have done?

SABIAN: You never really answered my question. How do you know when the world is ending? Is this the end, us here, now?

MARCUS: It's just us here now, Sabian. I think we can safely say the world as we knew it has ended.

We could go check on the perimeters, maybe we caught something in our traps to supplement the rations.

SABIAN: Yes—let's go.

If this is the end, why weren't people rioting in the streets before we got here?

Leaving while still talking.

MARCUS: Sabian, maybe they didn't have your cushion . . .

SCENE SIX

JESSICA: Marcus?

MARCUS: Jessica!

JESSICA: Do you have any extra rations? I mean, I know we have no extra anything here . . . I know this is out of the blue, and so much to ask, but I have to. Do you have them?

MARCUS: Sure—I mean, no. I don't have any extra, but you can share what I have. It's not like you to ask, so I know you must be really desperate.

JESSICA: Thank you!

Sits down, is obviously distracted and worried.

MARCUS: So . . . what's up, Jessica? You seem high-strung—like, more than your usual high-strung. This is a new level of edgy, even for you.

JESSICA: I just . . . found out some news and I am making a plan for the next few months. My ration supply is . . . late. Anyways, I'm fine. Thank you again.

Gets up to go.

MARCUS: You don't have to go, you know.

I mean, we are two people on an entire continent with what? Maybe thirty people here. Aren't you lonely?

JESSICA: I've been lonelier.

Sighs.

I am lonely. Do you have any coffee on? Shit, no—tea?

MARCUS: Sure.

You know what I miss most? Grass!

JESSICA: Your cannabis rations aren't coming in?

MARCUS: No! Like, actual grass—like, lying in the park under the cherry blossoms, or walking in tall grass in the field.

When we had to be worried about ticks. When insects were still teeming.

There's just been so many changes. It's breathtaking how fast it all happened.

JESSICA: I miss being warm. I miss grocery shopping. I used to go late at night, you know? No crowds, just me and my cart, aisle after aisle of food. Not rations, but actual food. While it lasted.

Sorry, I'm just nauseous. Or hungry. Or nauseous and hungry. Do you have peppermint tea?

MARCUS: We're gonna run out of rations soon. Have you thought any more about coming with us? I have my country's seed stores; we could start terraforming. Maybe the training won't have been completely useless.

JESSICA: No.

MARCUS: You're gonna need a plan.

JESSICA: And I'll make one. You know what—it is nausea. I'm just gonna go. Thank you for the rations.

MARCUS: Wait, don't leave without them—you know what, I'll bring them to you—this week. Just take care of yourself, okay?

JESSICA: Aren't you scared? You could die out there. We could die. Aren't you terrified?

MARCUS: I guess . . . I'm scared. But I'm more scared about what would happen if we don't act. Jess, we have a chance here. I'm gonna take it.

JESSICA: Well, thanks for the rations.

MARCUS: No. Wait, Jessica—stay. I'm scared too.

Jessica!

(trailing off) I'm scared too!

SCENE SEVEN

SABIAN: You know what? I was just thinking about when we were sent here, how we were sent to this wide white continent.

About how they actually called this place, our birthplace, the wide white continent.

Just like Canada—the great white north—I guess. Why are there so many places coded for white only?

Three of us Antarcticans were of colour. THREE of eleven. And some of us were already organizers. Okay, I was already an organizer.

But anyways, what did they think would happen when they sent a group of scrappy BIPOCS to colonize the wide white continent?

MARCUS: One—I'd hardly call Jessica scrappy, and two—you're being boastful already and we haven't even left. We could die out there you know.

If there's a storm, we're toast.

If our regulators tweak out, we'll freeze to death in the water.

We may never reach our goal. We have to swim for a week. I mean, we have the option of the flotation assist, but still. We might not make it. You get that, right?

SABIAN: We are going to make it. I know we will. As an activist I got a sense, like a tingling, when something was a really good plan, like, an action plan. And I have that feeling now. We can do this. We will be free.

MARCUS: Are you sure you're going to be okay leaving her?

SABIAN: What do you mean?

MARCUS: Jessica.

SABIAN: We've already discussed this. I'm fine. Why bring this up again?

MARCUS: C'mon, Sabian. I know. I know about how it is with you and Jessica. I have seen you in the same space. It's like electric. And she wouldn't come with you. And so we are actively leaving her. I just want to make sure you're okay—

SABIAN: Marcus. It's fine. Shit. We don't have time for this. Let's just get ready to go.

BOTH: What was that?

SABIAN: Fuck! There's a storm coming. We'll have to wait it out. We can't enter the waters now. This is such shitty timing.

BOTH: JESSICA!

JESSICA: I don't know what I'm doing here, but I'm here.

So, when do we leave?

SABIAN: After the storm.

ALL: It's the fucking tarps.

MARCUS: Let's go retie them.

JESSICA: Why are we here, little one?

Giggling.

Little one. We're here.

I came because of you. We're gonna try to go and be freer together. I have no idea if we'll make it, but I'm gonna do everything to keep you safe.

You'll be the first free-born Antarctican. Born of two women, strong together.

I don't know if the thermal regulators will keep us safe . . . And swimming for a week sounds like hell . . . but I guess I am in my second trimester now, so I'm stronger than I've ever been.

FUCK! I need to tell them about you. But I'm not ready.

We're not ready . . . I can't imagine what the company will do when they find out about you. Would do . . . they must ever know. We must keep you safe, little one, out from under their watch.

I never meant to get messed up with an activist. She's everything I am not.

Maybe that is precisely WHY it's going to work.

She laughs.

Fuck, now I sound like Sabian! The tarps!

SCENE EIGHT

SABIAN: The fires have been raging for over a year now, it's amazing that there is anything left to burn on this earth. My government stopped sending rations exactly four months ago. I presume they have been consumed by the fires. It's the only thing that makes sense.

DEAFY
BY CHRIS DODD

INTRODUCTION
BY DR. JENELLE ROUSE

"You will find as you look back upon your life that the moments when you have truly lived are the moments when you have done things in the spirit of love."
—Henry Drummond, 1851–1897

Moments (memories) in life are precious and special. We each have them to relive with a nostalgic feeling regardless of how significant or insignificant the memories may be. As a culturally Deaf artist with an authentic and intellectual fascination for languages (linguistics), I begin the discussion of this play with its title: *Deafy*. When looking at the word chosen for this play by Chris Dodd, I wonder what the title really means.

I take a close look at a picture of a white cis male holding up his left hand forming a manual letter in American Sign Language (ASL), "D."

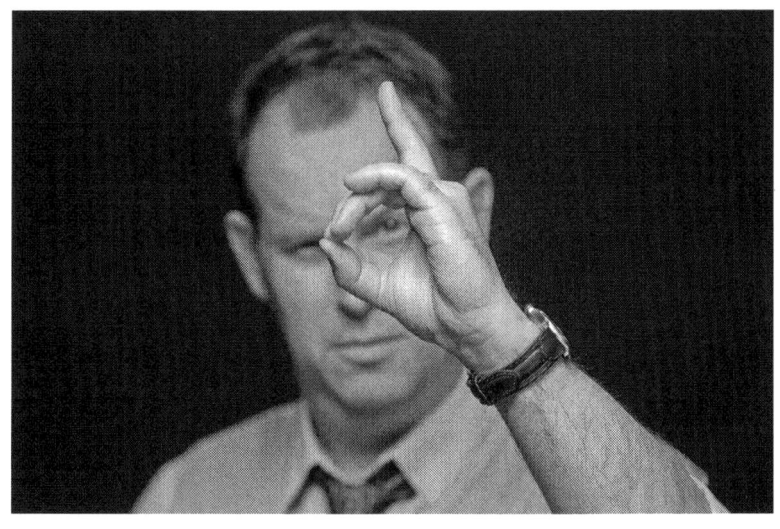

Photo of Chris Dodd by Marc J. Chalifoux.

The letter, "D," does represent *Deaf*, and the play is about Deaf individuals' life experiences. However, I must pause and look at how he positions the letter. Perhaps he is communicating more than the letter because he puts it in front of his face. I look at the picture again and, suddenly, I feel compelled to draw a specific hand to analyze a seemingly obvious yet somehow subtle meaning behind the letter.

There it is! An eye behind the "D" letter. Taking a much closer look at the eye, what does it want to tell us about the play?

Sketch by Dr. Jenelle Rouse, *Multi-Lens Existence.*

The play is inviting us into the *Deafy* world to meet a character—white, cis male, Deaf settler named Nathan. He is a proud Deaf Canadian. Nathan travels internationally as a professional lecturer. On the stage, Nathan courageously shares his heart-wrenching journey about his experience as a Deaf person living in the assimilated, abled, hearing world. Nathan's story brings members of an audience to an awareness of a historic issue that continues to exist in Deaf communities in the twenty-first century: *audism*.[1]

Audism is a term reflecting a person (whether they are Deaf or hearing) holding an erroneous notion that having an ability to hear and/or speak would lead to a better life, better opportunities, better job, and many other "betters." The play encourages the audience to take a careful look at the significant matters of human rights and dignity of those who are Deaf while removing the notion of deafness as a deficit.

Back to Nathan's eye behind his hand: What does he see? What is he trying to tell us? Is Nathan's story going to be warm and inviting? Or is it going to be scary? While it is up to the audience to decide the genre of the play, they may find it simply mysterious and romantic. Ultimately, the play is raw, emotionally charged for individuals who may go through

---

1 For further examples and definitions of audism, see Bauman; Eckert and Rowley; Humphries; and Lane.

Cropped sketch by Dr. Jenelle Rouse, *Multi-Lens Existence.*

what Nathan has gone through. Nathan's story enables the audience members to develop or strengthen their sensitivity or openness to an understanding of what it means to a Deaf person to be treated with dignity and be seen as human.

Nathan tells his story by code-switching between ASL, artificial sign system (Total Communication,[2] in particular), and speaking (English). By code-switching, he attempts to build a bridge between two languages and two cultures simultaneously to communicate his experience with every member of the audience. Nathan may do this to please them, because he seeks to *belong or be accepted.*

Belonging. Acceptance. Humanity.

Nathan lives in two worlds and cultures: Deaf and hearing. Are these worlds/cultures separate, or do they collide when languages are involved? How could Nathan know which world or culture he truly belongs to? Why is there a need for him to belong? Has Nathan found a shared linguistic ownership of, for example, a sense of pride; a sense of belonging; and a sense of knowing who he is? Does he know where he comes from and why he chooses to stay? Must he choose whether to commute between or abandon any of these worlds or cultures?

Although the play mainly intersects with those hearing members in the audience, Deaf members are encouraged to engage. The play belongs to everyone. It is critical for individuals to observe how they react to Nathan's story. That is, how do they react or behave when Nathan faces or survives different types of challenges such as bullying, favouritism, and hierarchy? Or even worse, being ignored? Do they care what happens to Nathan in the play?

---

2   To be precise, Total Communication (TC) is defined by Sue Schwartz as "a manual sign system [used] simultaneously [. . .] with speech" (Schwartz 91).

"Identity or linguistic profiling" probably is a perfect phrase to use to describe what is really happening to Nathan as he journeys through society in the play. The audience needs to be reminded that they should not, as per the old adage, "judge a book by its cover." They need to observe the first impressions Nathan has for himself and other people he meets or mingles with. In other words, audience members need to be conscious with how they judge Nathan's story.

Furthermore, this play is a chance for the audience to pause and actively unpack their opinions by asking themselves questions as follows:

- Is there a stigma around being "Deaf"? If so, why?
- Have I changed who I am in order to feel a sense of belonging to a community?
- Would I rebel against having to assimilate? If so, how would I do that?
- If I experienced such misunderstandings or miscommunications, what would I do?
  - Would I turn away?
  - Would I face them and move forward?

This show is educational and relatable for anyone who has had the experience of wanting to belong or of taking risks in response to challenges as per their natural curiosity. Go to the play and be taken into the *Deafy* world! The show is accessible to everyone as it is fully surtitled and includes the incorporation of ASL, artificial sign system, and English.

REFERENCES

Bauman, H.L. "Audism: Exploring the Metaphysics of Oppression." *The Journal of Deaf Studies and Deaf Education* 9, no. 2 (2004): 239–46. https://doi.org/10.1093/deafed/enh025.

Drummond, Henry. "Henry Drummond Quotes." https://www.brainyquote.com/quotes/henry_drummond_100712.

Eckert, Richard Clark, and Rowley, Amy June. "Audism: A Theory and Practice of Audiocentric Privilege." *Humanity & Society* 37, no. 2 (2013): 101–30. https://doi.org/10.1177/0160597613481731.

Humphries, T. "Audism: The Making of a Word." 1975. Unpublished essay.

———. "Communicating Across Cultures (Deaf/Hearing) and Language Learning." Union Graduate School, Cincinnati, 1977. Unpublished dissertation.

Lane, Harlan. "Oppression in the Relationship Between Hearing Professionals and the Culturally Deaf." *New Social Practices* 6, no. 1 (1993): 41–56. https://doi.org/10.7202/301195ar.

Schwartz, Sue. *Choices in Deafness: A Parent's Guide to Communication Options*. Woodbine House, 1996.

PLAYWRIGHT'S NOTE

Deaf identity is a complex thing. This is especially true for the protagonist of *Deafy*, Nathan Jesper, as he navigates his intricate existence between the hearing and Deaf worlds.

In reflection of the play's name, the word "deaf" occurs repeatedly on nearly every page of the script. During the writing of this play, I made a deliberate decision to treat this word as any other and I have left it in lower case without any consideration of its political implications.

The word is regularly capitalized to signal an attachment to the culture and community of the Deaf and used in lower case to indicate audiological status and those who might not identify with that community.

However, there is no one way of being deaf or Deaf. Deafness is a spectrum that involves varying degrees of hearing ability, the use (or not) of verbal speech, and degrees of proficiency in sign language. As well, this identity can be shaped or mired by the individual's education, social circles, and their families and their attitudes, especially toward the use of sign language.

Given that capitalization can be a loaded way of indicating allegiance and identity, I wanted the word to stand on its own in the play without needing to add additional baggage to Nathan's actions and words. After all, Nathan's struggles are complex enough.

Deafy premiered at the SummerWorks Performance Festival at the Theatre Centre on August 9th, 2019, in a co-production between Follow the Signs Theatre and Why Not Theatre with the following cast:

Nathan Jesper: Chris Dodd

Directed by Ashley Wright
Sound design by Darrin Hagen and Dave Clarke
Surtitles design by Milane Pridmore-Franz
Video design by Matt Schuurman
ASL coaching by Amorena Bartlett

A mostly bare stage. A podium sits off to the side downstage and nearby upstage is a wooden stool. NATHAN *Jesper can be seen in the middle of the stage lying on the floor on his back with his eyes closed. After a moment,* NATHAN *slowly stirs and then opens his eyes. Suddenly, he bolts upright and jumps to his feet with his back to the audience. As he turns, he is startled to see the audience there. He approaches them and begins to sign rapid fire. After a few moments,* NATHAN *senses the audience does not understand what he is signing and he stops.* NATHAN's *dialogue from this point will be spoken, signed, and projected in surtitles, unless otherwise indicated.*

NATHAN: Who are you?

Deaf?

Hearing?

You people are mostly hearing, right?

Want me to sign too? Okay, all right.

NATHAN looks around. Shift.

Oh, shit! Where are the interpreters? Did they book them?

Beat.

I was told there would be captions.

NATHAN turns and sees the captions at the rear wall.

Testing. Testing. One, two three . . .

NATHAN suddenly spins around, trying to catch the captions off guard.

Testing!

He spins again.

Testing!

Okay, listen, I'm sorry I'm late. It wasn't my fault. I got bumped. It happens.

NATHAN notices the podium downstage. He fetches it and places it centre stage. He feels around in his pockets and discovers his index cards, which he looks through.

Okay. All right, all right. We can still do this . . . this presentation.

Okay. Let's get this back on track.

NATHAN prepares himself and then begins his speech. During the following lines, his voice is markedly different and he sounds very monotone. He becomes increasingly uncomfortable as he progresses through his speech.

Thank you for coming today. Allow me to introduce myself. My name is Nathan Jesper and I'll be your presenter tonight. I want to begin by listing some important facts about deafness. Right.

Firstly, approximately one in every four Canadians has some degree of hearing loss. However, not everyone with hearing loss identifies as being deaf or hard of hearing. Some people . . . just want to be themselves.

Secondly, sign languages are not universal. There are over one hundred unique sign languages around the world. Which, when you think about it, gives you one hundred different ways of saying, "Up yours."

Thirdly, not everyone who is Deaf or hard of hearing knows sign language. Some do, some don't. Usually people who identify as hard of hearing are less likely to sign. Okay?

Fourth, a common misconception is that a person who is Deaf cannot speak. Fact: many people who are Deaf can speak to some degree.

(speaks only, articulating) Including . . . people . . . like . . . me, . . . right?

> NATHAN's *discomfort has reached its breaking point and he can no longer continue. He abruptly leaves the podium, breathing heavily. After a moment, he spots a stool off to the side. He looks at the audience and then back at the stool. He fetches it and places it behind the podium. He lifts the podium and returns it to where he found it and then returns and sits on the stool.* NATHAN's *tone shifts.*

Let me tell you about my friend Len. Len's deaf like me. I think he has it worse because he's not as good a lip-reader as I am. He thinks that the hearing community is out to get him. He often says, "Hearing people are crazy."

> *A house light blinks.*

What? Yeah, I know I'm going off-script. Honestly, I don't care! You know what? I'm tired of giving the same old talk. Tonight, I'm just going to tell them like it is. Okay?

There was this bar that Len used to go to. Len's a sports kind of guy and he loves his hockey. Since Len doesn't have cable at home, he needs to go out to a bar every time he wants to watch a game. Except—get this—he's a Maple Leafs fan. Can you believe it?

I say to him, "Len, how can you support the Maple Leafs? You've never been to Toronto. And they're the worst team in the world."

And he told me, "Shows what you know. You always gotta root for the underdogs. 'Cause if I don't, who will?"

So, anyways, Len always goes to this bar because it's just a couple of blocks from his house. Respectable place, nothing too fancy. Never that busy. The usual sports stuff hanging on the walls and a good number of TVs over the bar. They always have them turned on to the hockey game, so Len's happy about that. But—get this—the captions on the TVs aren't on.

Len tried to ignore this for a while. But after a few games of this and a lot of grumbling from him, I finally convince him to go up to the bar. The bartender tells him there's nothing he could do and Len needs to talk with the manager. But the manager's not there.

So, the next day, me and Len head back to the bar and we talk with the manager. He's this burly guy named Gary. Gary tells him, "Nope. Can't do that. The other customers will complain."

Len swears up and down that he's never gonna go back to that bar again. He's finished with that place. But Len doesn't drive and the next closest sports bar is thirty minutes by bus and he's too cheap to take a cab.

So, the next day, Len goes back to the bar, complains about the captions again. Guess what? Yep, he gets shot down again.

But Len doesn't give up. He's the kinda guy who will walk for fifteen minutes back to Tim Hortons if they give him a stale cup of coffee. Day after day, Len would show up, complain about the captions, and each time he would get shot down and told there was nothing they could do. In spite of this, Len would still buy a beer and sulk in the corner and try to follow the game.

This went on for weeks.

Then one day Len walked into the bar and every single TV in the whole place was lit up with captions. And also, the place was packed! It turns out that they hired a new chef from this hip restaurant on the other side of town and the word got around. Not only that, everyone in the bar now seemed to enjoy the captions because they could follow the games no matter how loud it got.

A little while after this, I bumped into Len. I asked him how he was enjoying the change.

He told me, "I stopped going to that place."

"What? Len, you went there for weeks and complained every day. After all that trouble, you finally got what you wanted. Why would you stop going?"

"Well, for one thing, now there's too many hearing people."

And Len thought hearing people were the CRAZY ones.

> *The projector gets stuck on the word "crazy" and it does not fade out with the rest of the words.*

Let's talk about communication . . .

> NATHAN *senses something is wrong and turns around.*

Hey, captions!

The word fades.

Projection: SORRY.

NATHAN *regards this but decides to ignore it.*

Let's talk about communication . . .

Of course, many people who are deaf can communicate through lip-reading. Which leads me to the most common question I get when I meet a new person for the first time:

(speaks only) "Do . . . you . . . read . . . lips?"

Let's look at the two ways I could answer this question.

One: I could say "yes."

But then the person thinks, "Aha! This is so easy!" and then they proceed to start babbling away with their lips, chewing on their pencils, covering their mouths, moving their heads around, and doing all that kind of stuff.

And then you have to say, "Oh, no, no. Hold on a minute! Yes, I read lips. But—"

And the other person interrupts, *(speaks only)* "Oh, I'm sorry! Would . . . it . . . help . . . if . . . I . . . spoke . . . more . . . slowly?"

And then you have to interrupt. "No, listen. You don't need to speak slowly. You only need to speak clearly."

And then they will raise their voice.

Every time. Every goddamned time!

Okay, maybe I don't know when they are raising their voice because I can't hear them. But if we're out in public and people start turning their heads and gawking at us, then I know one of us is speaking loudly AND I DON'T THINK IT'S ME!

Now, if I say, "No, I can't read lips," what do you think happens then?

Everything stops.

Their face . . . It's frozen. Uncomprehending. It's like there's this chasm that suddenly opens up beneath our feet, hundreds of miles deep, and the earth tears us asunder. There we stand, separated by the vast distance, until one of us finally turns around and walks away.

>   NATHAN *shoots his hand straight up and snaps his fingers. Lights shift to a spot just on him. Speaks only.*

You,
face-to-face,
alone,
with a fully deaf person
and no means of communication.
No pen,
no phone,
no sign language,
and no help.

>   *He snaps again and the lights return.*

Len announced to me one day that he thought I should learn to drive.

I asked him, "Why don't YOU learn to drive?"

He told me there wasn't any point. He didn't own a car and couldn't afford the insurance. So that left me, since I had my father's '85 Cutlass

Supreme sitting in the garage, which he gave me five years back. I never drove it on account of only having a learner's permit.

So me and Len go down to the registry office. We take a ticket from the dispenser and we sit on the benches and wait.

When it was our turn, we go up to the counter and hand our ticket to a heavy-set woman with thin lips. She takes my learner's license and starts punching the info into the computer.

While we're waiting, me and Len start joking around, only we're not speaking, just signing.

Suddenly, out of the corner of my eye, I see her large arms waving frantically.

"Excuse me, sir! Are you hearing impaired?"

For a moment, I'm not sure how to answer this. Did she not see me signing with Len? Is it not clearly obvious that I am a person who is deaf?

I'm trying to think of some witty retort but it's taking too long, so I just say:

"No, I'm not 'hearing impaired.' I'm deaf, actually."

She does a bit of a stutter and her face jerks and twists as she tries to process this information.

It's almost as if I was a blind guy who walked into the cockpit of a jumbo jet and asked if I could please have a try at landing the plane.

She says, rather loudly, or I think it was loud, "I'm sorry, sir. I'm not allowed to issue a license to someone who is deaf."

This sets Len off. He starts yelling:

"Listen, lady! As long as there have been cars, deaf people have been driving them! Deaf people drive trains! Deaf people fly planes! Deaf people ride bikes! Deaf people sail ships!

IF SOMETHING MOVES, A DEAF PERSON SOMEWHERE HAS DRIVEN IT!"

All this commotion causes the woman's supervisor to come out from the back to see what all the shouting is about. After the woman at the desk explains, he tells her she is, in fact, wrong and that deaf people CAN drive. She just needs to put the correct code in the database.

Len's smile goes from ear to ear while the woman's cheeks go from pink to deep red.

So, I pay the fee and the supervisor gives us the date and time for the driver's test for a week from today. Before we leave, I ask him if my interpreter will be in the front seat or in the back.

"I'm sorry, sir. It will be only you and the examiner. No one else is allowed in the car."

Can you believe it? I open my mouth and I'm just about to argue with him but Len grabs my elbow and leads me to the door.

He told me it's true. His friend Josh took his driver's test about a year back and they wouldn't let him have an interpreter either.

Josh is stone deaf and doesn't speak, so he couldn't communicate with the examiner once the test started. The examiner used a bunch of gestures to tell Josh what he wanted him to do but Josh got so confused that he ended up failing. The next time he tried, the examiner tried writing things down and showing it to him but that was almost a disaster because he was so distracted trying to read that he almost ran this old man over at a crosswalk.

By the time Josh finally got it right and passed the test, he was nearly four hundred dollars in the hole.

I tell Len this isn't going to work. There's no way I am spending that kind of money to get my license. Besides, I don't need to learn to drive that badly.

But Len isn't having any of it. He tells me, "Let's use Sarah."

Sarah is Len's friend. She has a deaf uncle, or something or another—someone in her family, I wasn't really paying attention. She's a little loopy but she's a decent signer.

Len's plan goes like this: Sarah will hide in the back of the car under a blanket. When the test starts, Sarah will slowly emerge behind the examiner and will stealthily interpret everything he says. Len says I just need to look in the rearview mirror and it will all be easy-peasy.

Of course, I think this plan is completely insane. But I've already paid eighty bucks for the test and I'm probably going to fail it anyways.

On the day of the test, I meet the examiner in the parking lot who introduces himself as Naveen. He dresses the part perfectly: button-up shirt, dark slacks, glasses, and black running shoes. He carries a clipboard.

He walks around the car and does the pre-check. While he is doing this, out of the corner of my eye, I see the blanket shift in the back seat. I look over at Naveen but, luckily, he didn't see it.

We get in the car and pull out of the parking lot and start down the street.

On cue, Sarah slowly emerges behind the examiner and I see her in the rearview mirror. The examiner is speaking and using gestures and I am able to follow Sarah in the mirror signing to me.

For the first while, it's all good. I'm changing lanes, using my blinkers, doing my shoulder-checks. The parallel parking part bit comes and I pretty much nail it. At this point, I'm feeling good about things.

And that's where it all goes *wrong*.

Naveen figures by this time he doesn't need to verbalize his directions, since I can't hear him anyways. So, he starts giving directions with just gestures. But Sarah can't see his gestures because he's in front of her.

I'm trying to figure out who I should be paying attention to and I'm looking between Naveen and Sarah in the rear-view mirror but Sarah is no longer any help. Naveen notices I'm distracted and starts gesturing more urgently. However, I'm becoming stressed and I can't focus on what he's trying to tell me.

Naveen grabs his pen and hurriedly starts writing. At that moment, the ever-so-helpful Sarah pops her head around from the back so she can read it too. But she forgot she's not supposed to be there!

Naveen sees Sarah and lets out a terrified scream. This startles Sarah who also starts screaming. I start screaming, mostly because everyone else in the car is screaming.

Because I have two screaming and panicking people in the car, I veer right off the road, over a stop sign and through a wooden fence before coming to a stop in front of a plastic garden gnome.

> *Sound FX, tires squealing, crash of metal on metal and metal on wood. Lights flicker and then blackout.*

Hey! Lights! Lights!

> *They come back on.*

Now, listen. I don't expect you to believe this—but deaf people really are better drivers.

For one thing, we don't listen to the radio. And don't get me started about people talking on their phones.

Driving favours the eyes and not the ears. You've heard it said that when people lose one sense, the others become stronger. Let me tell you, it's totally true. As long as I have good eyesight, I'm always going to be a good driver. Which is why I'm not looking forward to getting old.

But it's kind of funny when you think about it, because all of you will probably be a bit deaf later in life. Maybe you'll be better drivers then.

But then again maybe not, because you'll probably still be on your phones.

> *A deep rumbling is heard through the theatre.* NATHAN *senses it, even though he can't hear it.*

What?

What is it?

> *The lights in the wings of stage right suddenly jump to full, bathing* NATHAN *in bright, white light. This startles* NATHAN *and he instinctively shields himself, protecting his body.*

HEY! CUT IT OUT!

> *The wing lights fade.*

Listen, I don't need this right now! I woke up late and then I rushed to the airport, only to get bumped.

Beat.

Let me tell you about the last time I rode the train.

So, I'm at the far end of the car, minding my own business, and then at the other end I see this guy with this old accordion. He's dressed how you would expect an accordion player to look. Bow tie, vest, hat with a feather—the whole shebang.

He starts playing this lively and melodic song while he walks down the aisle. Okay, maybe I don't know if it was melodic or not but clearly this guy was doing something right, because everyone's attention is focused on him.

He's smiling this big smile that reaches from one end of the car to the other and fills it up with that grin of his. Soon everyone in the car is reflecting that smile back at him. Everyone's into it. The whole car is entranced by his music. He's got a bag tied to the side of his belt and everyone has got their purses and wallets out and they're pulling out bills and stuffing them into his bag.

I'm the mute witness to all this. Let me be completely honest with you. I always feel a bit guilty every time I pass a street musician, because, hey, they're out there trying to add a little cheer into people's dreary lives and hope that they feel inspired enough to give a few bucks.

But me? It's not doing anything for me, but they DON'T KNOW IT. Sometimes I want to yell out, "Sorry. Deaf!" as I walk past so they don't think I'm some soulless tightwad.

This, however, is different, because I'm stuck on this train with no place to go.

After a few minutes, he arrives where I am sitting. But instead of continuing on, he stops and looks right at me, still smiling. At this point, the song is cresting and he's playing even faster.

I'm probably the only person in the car who isn't smiling at this point. Also, I don't have my wallet out either. And this guy knows it—which is why he has me locked dead in his sights.

I can feel everyone looking at me. This guy has won over the whole car and he is absolutely NOT going to finish his song without a complete victory.

All of a sudden, everyone starts to clap. I don't mean applause—he's not finished yet. I mean the kind of clapping that musicians ask you to do to keep the beat with the music. Like this:

> *He claps above his head several times.*

(if audience starts clapping, retort) Oh, no, no! Don't clap!

The accordion guy is racing toward the finish of the song, still smiling his smile, eyes locked on me, his fingers working frantically, as everyone in the car cheers him on, clapping rhythmically. He gets down on his knees—his goddamned knees!—right in front of me as he finishes with a flourish.

The clapping stops. Dead silence.

Just then, the train pulls into the station and I jump from my seat and rush to the door.

Just before I exit through the door, I turn and pause for just enough time to yell out one single word, "DEAF!" before running off as fast as I could.

Like I said, that was the last time I ever rode the train.

> *There is a steady rhythmic heartbeat sound. The lights shift. The projection screen shows a heartbeat and* NATHAN *grabs his chest and contorts his face in pain. After a moment, the heartbeat*

fades out. The lights resume to a normal state and NATHAN *recovers.*

Beat.

Let me tell you about this one time I was at McDonald's.

So, I'm at the counter, all right? I'm waiting in line and there's this old lady in front of me. She's about five feet tall, skinny, white curls covering her head. She's wearing a pea-green coat, a plaid scarf, basic jeans, and white running shoes. She's buying a coffee.

She shuffles off slowly and I don't think too much more of it.

I get my order and then go and sit down. Just a moment after I do, the old lady comes over and sits next to me. Just like that. No invitation or anything.

She smiles and sets down her coffee. And then she starts talking to me.

I don't mean "talking" as in a how-do-you-do kind of way. I mean talking as in the words start spilling out of her mouth and it's like the faucet has broken off.

She's going on and on about something, but I can't understand what. She's speaking with barely any pauses and I can't get a word in. Maybe I remind her of her grandson or maybe she has something she wants to get off her chest, I don't know.

She goes on for five minutes straight and then, finally, she's finished.

With slow, unsteady hands, she takes the lid off her coffee, takes a sip, and then puts it down again. And then I realize that she is looking at me.

I could tell her that I'm deaf.

I could tell her that for the last five minutes she's been speaking to someone who has not heard or understood a single word she has said. But I don't. Instead I say:

"Yes, you're right."

Because why not? Doesn't everyone want to be told that they're right? Doesn't every person want and crave affirmation?

It doesn't matter if you are young, old, disabled, able-bodied, straight, queer, a person of minority, or a white privileged male, everyone wants to feel they are right. And why not her?

She starts speaking again but this time more steadily and less hurried. Every few sentences now, she pauses, and takes a sip of her coffee.

I start eating and I punctuate her pauses with nods of my head. In between these pauses I say:

"Uh-huh."

"Yes."

"I agree."

And, "You're right."

We go back and forth in this manner until I am all done eating and her cup is nearly empty.

Even though I didn't hear her, I feel I understand her. She's a lot like me. We're both a little lost, we're both a little alone.

Sometimes I just can't be bothered to connect with someone. There's no secret in that. But other times, like her, I just feel like I need to belong.

A few days later, Len came over to my house . . .

> *The rest of the words disappear but "BELONG" stays on projection screen.* NATHAN *senses something is wrong and looks back at the screen.*

Hey! Captions!

> *The word disappears.*

A few days later, Len came over to my house . . .

I thought that he had come over to hang around, drink some beers, play some Nintendo, like we always do. But the moment he came through my door and I saw the look on his face, I knew something was wrong.

I asked him, "What is it?"

"It's Sarah."

"What's that girl done now?"

"It's not her. Us. We're getting married."

This completely threw me. I always knew that Len and Sarah had a thing but I had no idea that it was serious. But then again, we had other things to chat about than relationships.

I start laughing, in spite of myself, imagining what kind of married couple those two were going to make. But then I realize that Len's not smiling. He's sitting there slumped on my armchair.

Before I can process this, Len tells me there is more.

He and Sarah are moving out of town, about three hours away. Sarah had gotten a new job through a family member, which, while not great, is better than her dead-end waitressing job.

Len says there's more. He's getting a cochlear implant.

"What?! Len! Why would you do that?"

He says Sarah thinks it would be a good idea. So does her family. Sarah's father said that there's no reason to suffer, yes, SUFFER, with having a disability like deafness when there is a cure for it.

Sarah's uncle is too old for the operation, so he never had it but the family all thinks he should have because all he does is sit around the house half-dressed in his robe and watch TV. He's never had a real job and he just farts around and collects EI.

Len says it is an easy operation and the government covers the cost. They put you on the table, they cut you open, jab some electrodes right into your brain, and then BOOM! Just like that. No more deafness!

You go in the hospital deaf and you walk out of those doors hearing. He said that her father knows all this because he works for the hospital of the Holy Cross of the Bleeding Mary or something or the other.

I try pleading with him. "But Len, you're a deaf person. This is YOU. This is your identity."

Len looks at me for a moment. I mean he really looks at me.

It's like he's weighing his words, percolating them, and it takes a moment for him to speak.

When he does, out spills all the reasons he hates being deaf. He tells me about being teased in school and how the other kids made fun of him because of his hearing aids.

He tells me about how he hates ordering at fast food restaurants because the clerks never understand him the first time and he winds up needing to repeat himself again and again.

He hates when he meets strangers and the struggles to communicate with them, and he hates it when people say they are "sorry" that he is deaf. He hates it when people look at him weird when he opens his mouth. He hates being left out; he hates not belonging. He hates sitting alone at parties and family gatherings with no one to talk to and being bored out of his mind.

He hates living in a world that is made for people with ears that hear, and which doesn't care one fucking bit about people with ears that don't.

We are both quiet for a moment. Len says he's done.

It's not about me but what he wants. And what Sarah wants. And what her family wants.

Sticking around here, he's not going anywhere, so he needs to move on with his life. And that means becoming a hearing person.

I don't know what else there is to say. Len's mind is made up. No amount of pleading or arguing with him will change that. But deep down, it really bugs me.

Me and Len walk to the door and say goodbye. I want to hug him. I want to grab him and hold onto him tight and not let go. But I know he would think that would be weird. I want to protect him, even though there's nothing to protect him from.

All I can do is watch him go. Len says that he will write, even though we both know that he won't. And then he is gone.

The lights change. The stage lights become dark with a single light focused on NATHAN. *On the screen, the words "*NATHAN, NATHAN*" appear. Although* NATHAN *does not see this, he still reacts to it.*

What? What is it?

Who is it?

Who's there?!

The words on the screen change to: "It's me."

Len? Is that you, Len?

Projector: "No, me."

You?

Projector: "Me."

A deep rumbling sound is heard. NATHAN, *disoriented, moves upstage. The lights in the wings jump to full, blinding* NATHAN.

But—No! Wait, wait . . . You can't—

The rumbling subsides and lights return. NATHAN *pauses for a moment and recovers.*

Beat.

I tried to move on after Len left. Without him, the centre had fallen through, leaving this vast empty void of friendship, and there was almost nothing left.

So, I start to hang out with Josh. Remember Josh? Len's stone-deaf friend. I didn't really know him that well, but me and Len hung around with him on occasion.

So, I text Josh and we make plans to meet up the following Saturday. He lives in a suite in his parent's basement on the other side of town.

When I get there, a bunch of Josh's other friends have already arrived. They are all deaf themselves. They've all been friends since elementary because they all went to the same deaf school the next town over.

Josh introduces me to each person with rapid finger-spelling of their name along with an equally rapid demonstration of their sign names.

There's Donny, a skinny guy with slicked dark hair who always wears a jean jacket.

Lyle, who, on account of having rich parents, always dresses in button-up shirts and slacks.

Zeke, with the big hair, the sole female in the group who always looks bored out of her mind.

And Brant, who I later learned to hate, is the prankster who always tries to get under everyone's skin.

Josh's big plan for the day is just to hang out. Okay, fine.

Josh has got a two-four, so we crack open some beers and sit around on his second-hand couches and beaten armchairs and watch TV with the captions on.

It's not much different than what I did with Len. However, there are a lot more people than I am used to and it's hard to keep up with the conversation. Everyone is signing rapid fire about events for which

I was not there and about people, and their name signs, whom I do not know.

It's like everyone is speaking a different dialect and every time someone talks about something or someone that I don't understand it takes me a minute to figure out what and who they are talking about.

Nobody really asks me anything about me. Every time I ask someone a question, I only get a quick response before someone else grabs their attention.

After a few hours, people start to head off. I ask Josh if he wants to hang out next week. I get only a one-word response:

(signs only) "Sure."

Okay, fine.

I head over to Josh's house the next week and it's more of the same thing.

I sit around and drink, and watch TV, while everyone else is a blur of rapid-fire signing about topics I don't understand and stories that I can't follow.

It's like six pairs of arms have taken over the room, waving, signing, finger-spelling, and filling the air with signals that bounce off each corner and then are lost as quickly as they appeared, only to be replaced by more.

Zeke is saying something about her mother's surgery, although I don't know what it was for.

Donny is talking about his motorcycle, but I don't know why.

Josh is complaining about something his parents did, but I don't know what.

Lyle is talking about how he quit his job, or maybe got fired; I can't tell which.

Brant is the only one I understand, but it turns out that he is making fun of my shoes.

Okay, fine.

A few days after this, I text Josh and ask if he wants to see a movie. It takes him awhile to text back, and when he does, he's noncommittal about it, so nothing comes out of it.

I'm busy the following weekend, so I don't meet up with Josh or his friends. So, a little while after, I text him and invite him, and this time everyone else, out to grab dinner on Wednesday. However, Josh doesn't text me back. So, a day later, I text him again. Nothing.

Okay, fine.

Awhile after this, I spot Josh in the street and I flag him down. I ask him if he got my texts.

(signs only) "Oh, yeah. Was busy."

If there's one thing, just one thing, you need to know about deaf people, it's the fact that we love our phones.

Phones are our link to the outside world and everyone in it. Texting, email, FaceTime, Instant Messenger, Facebook, Snapchat, Twitter, Instagram. We're connected like we've never been before.

Josh walks around with his phone glued to his hand. Half the time I am with him, he is holding his phone in one hand and signing to me with the other.

So, for him to say that he was too busy to check the phone that was already in his hand and type me a response is complete horseshit.

But I don't say this. I decide to ignore it and ask about getting together at his place the coming weekend. Josh's response is this:

(signs only) "Nah. That's fine."

My forehead starts to get hot and I feel a trickle of sweat down my back. I start to respond, but I don't really know what I say. What do you say when someone tells you they don't want to be your friend? Maybe this kind of thing was easier when you were a kid but as a grown-up it is incredibly embarrassing.

The only thing I can think of at the time is to ask: "Why?"

Josh responds:

> NATHAN *signs only, giving emphasis to each word, as the words appear on the screen one by one.*

"You're not deaf."

For a moment, I don't understand what he means. Of course I'm deaf! I have been hard of hearing since age six and fully deaf since age twelve. I haven't heard a thing in over twenty years. Why would he say that I am not deaf?

Then it comes to me. What Josh means is that I am not deaf ... enough. I wasn't born deaf. I don't have deaf parents. I didn't go to a deaf school. I'm not as graceful a signer as some of his friends are.

But what really hurts about this is that some of Josh's friends wear hearing aids. They listen to music and they are always talking about their favourite artists and they post videos online where they sign along with their favourite songs.

To Josh, they're deaf. And me—who doesn't even have enough hearing to even hear a fucking fire alarm—I am not.

So fuck that. I walk away. I don't see Josh ever again. Or any of his friends. I don't need friends like that.

A while later I got contacted by this woman, Julia. She was looking for an outreach representative for the Council of Deaf Canadians. They wanted to know if I would be interested in the job.

Why would they even want me? I had no idea. Even though I wasn't "deaf," apparently I was deaf enough to be qualified to explain it to hearing people.

The best part about that job was that I had to travel. Half the time I would be flying around the world, jumping from place to place, giving presentations, before coming home and then doing it all over again.

Of course I said yes. Because there was nothing here for me.

What is better than to have an opportunity to run away from your problems? To be able to fly away to where no one knows you, where no one judges you, and where no one will be around long enough to hurt you.

I don't need people. I don't need friends. I don't need anyone. All I need is me.

>   *Projection: "But it wasn't enough."*

Who the hell are you? What do you even know about it?

>   *Projection: "I'm me."*

Oh yeah? Well, why don't you tell the story?

Projection: "Tell them why."

Tell them why what?

Projection: "Why it wasn't enough."

It was enough! It WAS.

Okay. It was at first.

After a while of doing that job, I started to realize what it meant to just be me. I would meet people, but I would only know them for a day or two at the most. It wasn't long enough to make any kind of meaningful connection.

Even if I did connect with someone, it was pretty unlikely that I would be back any time soon. Little by little, I was withdrawing into myself and I stopped trying. I started to eat my lunches alone. I turned down opportunities to go for dinner or for drinks.

I just went and did my presentations and then went back to my hotel. And then the next day I would fly out and do the whole damned thing over again.

Projection: "Tell them about the man."

At the airport?

Projection: "Yes."

I don't want to tell that story.

Projection: "You have to."

Says who?

> Projection: "Nathan, you need to tell the story."
>
> A pause. NATHAN approaches the audience.

I flew into the airport late the night I saw him.

It was much later than I had planned. I had a presentation earlier that day and I was already tired. And I was already in a lousy mood.

I was sitting down on a bench in the terminal when I saw him across from me. Normally I don't stare at people. But when I saw him, I couldn't take my eyes off him.

He was sitting there. He had a long white beard, dark shoes, and a dark shirt. He had three suitcases, which were piled high on a cart.

But instead of being ready to go places, he looked like he was not going any place.

After a minute I realized he must be homeless. Here was a man who had no destination, no passport, and no place to be. A man without a country. A man who doesn't belong. A man just like me.

As my breathing became ragged, I quickly picked up my suitcase and ran as fast as I could. I had to get away.

I only made it a short distance and then found I could not run any further, and I collapsed to floor, sobbing.

I held myself as everything hit me all at once. Len leaving. Josh and his friends. The lonely old woman I met at McDonalds. Me trying to leave everything behind. Trying to be a man who doesn't belong.

> Projection: "Nathan, tell them about the car."

No.

Projection: "Nathan, the car."

No!

Projection: "Tell the story."

I don't want to!

Projection: "The car."

I didn't hear the car. All right? I mean, COME ON! I'm DEAF!

I wasn't . . . I wasn't trying to . . . I didn't mean to . . . Believe me. You have to believe me.

When I walked out of the terminal, I was still in shock. There were still tears in my eyes.

When I stepped off the curb, I thought I was paying attention. No, I didn't hear it. But maybe I saw it. I don't know.

Maybe I thought about . . . it. Just for a brief instant, when both time and space slowed down until they were almost frozen, I thought during that moment, "Maybe this is it."

This is the end.

This is my . . . freedom.

The end of heartbreak.

The end of being alone.

During the time the car was travelling toward me, I would have just enough time to close my eyes, and myself and everything . . . could disappear.

I remember the headlights, how they glowed across my body, illuminating me for all the world to see.

I'm sure they tried to brake. The impact was sickening. I remember the tremendous pain and being thrown, falling and tumbling through the air.

And then after that, nothing. Blackness.

> *There is a long silence.*

> *Projection: "The time has come."*

I know.

> *Projection: "Are you ready?"*

Yes.

> *There is a musical interlude.* NATHAN *slowly picks up the stool and returns it to its original position. He returns to centre stage and lies on the floor and closes his eyes. Patterns and shapes flood the screen, familiar yet strange, without any discernible pattern or meaning. Both music and lights fade, leaving* NATHAN *alone in silence. After a moment, he stirs as if waking from deep slumber. Upon opening his eyes, he shoots upright and jumps to his feet with his back to the audience. On turning, he is startled to discover the audience watching him. He walks toward them and studies them, regarding but not comprehending.*

Who are you?

> *Blackout.*

> *End of play.*

ABOUT THE CONTRIBUTORS

An award-winning writer, theatre maker, actor, and educator, and named one of the most influential disabled artists by UK's *Power Magazine*, **Alex Bulmer** has over thirty professional years of experience across theatre, film, television, radio, and education. She is dedicated to collaborative art practice, fuelled by a curiosity of the improbable, and deeply informed by her experience of becoming blind. Alex is the former artistic director of Common Boots Theatre, co-founder and artistic director of Cripping the Stage, and is lead curator of CoMotionFestival 2022, an international disability arts festival with Harbourfront Centre. She is the writer of the award-winning BBC adaptation of *The Hunchback of Notre Dame*, of *Breathe* and *The Garden*, both produced at the London and Rio Olympics, of the Dora Mavor Moore and Chalmers Award–nominated *Smudge*, and co-writer of the BAFTA-nominated UK television series *Cast Offs*, featuring six lead disabled actors. Alex earned best actor accolades at the Moscow International Disability Film Festival and recently completed a season as the Friar in *Romeo and Juliet* at the Stratford Festival.

Chris Dodd is an Edmonton-based Deaf actor for the stage and screen, playwright, consultant, accessibility advocate, and Governor General's Innovation Award finalist. He is the founder and artistic director of SOUND OFF, Canada's national theatre festival dedicated to the Deaf performing arts that takes place annually in Edmonton. His other plays include *Please Remain Behind The Shield*, commissioned by the SummerWorks Performance Festival and Canadian Stage, and *Alicia and the Machine*, which was commissioned by Concrete Theatre. Notable performances include *Ultrasound* at Theatre Passe Muraille. Chris holds a degree from the University of Alberta's drama program. In 2019 he was the recipient of the Guy Laliberté Prize for innovation and creative leadership from the Canada Council for the Arts.

ABOUT THE CONTRIBUTORS

Becky Gold is an accessible drama instructor, creative enabler, audio describer, and PH.D. candidate in Theatre and Performance Studies at York University in Toronto. She holds an Honours BA in Drama and English from Queen's University and an MA in Theatre Studies from the University of British Columbia. Her SSHRC-funded research explores disability-driven and interabled artistic practice, with a focus on the value of interdependence, relation-building, care, and access-intimacy in the creative process. Becky has also been published in the *Journal of Public Pedagogies*, *Frontiers: A Journal of Women Studies*, and *Studies in Social Justice*.

Andrew Gurza is an award-winning Disability Awareness Consultant Content Creator. He is the host of *Disability After Dark: The Podcast Shining a Bright Light on Disability Stories*, which won a Canadian Podcast Award in 2021. Andrew is also the creator of the viral hashtag #DisabledPeopleAreHot. You can find out more about Andrew by going to www.andrewgurza.com and connecting with him on social media at @andrewgurza_.

Ken Harrower is an actor and writer. He's been acting since 2011 in both films and theatre. He helped write *Access Me* along with the other main actors. He is currently working on a stage play about growing up in foster care and coming out as a gay disabled guy. He is very proud of *Access Me*! He has starred in two short films and plans to be acting and writing till he dies.

Frank Hull is an established, professional artist who proudly lives with cerebral palsy and madness, embraces his Mi'kmaq heritage, and celebrates his gay identity. Originally a choir vocalist, over the past fifteen years Hull has distinguished himself as one of Canada's most prominent power wheelchair choreographers and dancers. He more recently expanded his repertoire to include live and digital performance. Hull's artistic practice is multidisciplinary, consisting of varied, vibrant works in dance, theatre, music, and media arts. His artistic vision is to reveal the impacts of trauma and oppression on the body while positioning "deviant" bodies as a source of aesthetic appreciation, beauty, and enrichment.

Hull's dance works have been presented several times at Art With Attitude (Toronto). His most recent work includes contributing to *Access Me*, a play developed by the Boys in Chairs Collective, Toronto.

Yousef Kadoura was born in the midwestern United States and raised in Ottawa, Ontario. He is a Lebanese Canadian actor, writer, producer, as well as a right leg below knee amputee. Yousef is a graduate of the 2017 acting program at the National Theatre School of Canada. Since moving to Toronto from Montreal in 2017, he has worked as the curator-in-residence at Tangled Art + Disability, co-curating the Flourishing series in 2018. He is a producer, creator, and host of the podcast series *Crip Times*. Yousef is also a founding company member of Other HeArts, a new performance collective that came together initially as a producing vehicle for Yousef's show, *One Night*, in Aluna Theatre's 2019 CAMINOS festival. As an artist, Yousef seeks to draw from a plurality of experiences and disciplines to expand the boundaries of performance in pursuit of accessibility, presence, and shared experience.

Debbie Patterson is a Winnipeg playwright, director, and actor. Trained at the National Theatre School of Canada, she is a founding member of Shakespeare in the Ruins (SIR), served as Theatre Ambassador for Winnipeg's Cultural Capital year, and was Artistic Director of the Popular Theatre Alliance of Manitoba. She was the Carol Shields Writer-in-Residence (2012) at the University of Winnipeg and playwright-in-residence at Theatre Projects Manitoba in 2013/14. She served as Artistic Associate at Prairie Theatre Exchange (PTE) from 2012 to 2018 and is a member of the PTE Playwrights Unit. She is in demand across the country as a consultant on crip aesthetics/accessibility and as a dramaturge versed in disability aesthetics. She was honoured with the United Nations Platform for Action Committee's 2014 Activist Award and the Winnipeg Arts Council Making a Mark Award in 2017. She was twice shortlisted for the Gina Wilkinson Prize. She is a proud advocate for disability justice through her work as founding and current artistic director of Sick + Twisted Theatre. She lives a wheelchair-enabled life in Winnipeg and in a cabin on the shore of Lake Winnipeg with her partner and collaborator, Arne MacPherson.

ABOUT THE CONTRIBUTORS

Brian Postalian (Բրայն Փոսթալյան) is an arts administrator, educator, and creator born and raised in Toronto/Tkaronto by way of Armenia, Ireland, Wales, and the Czech Republic. As the founding artistic director of Re:Current Theatre, Brian creates collaborative performances in immersive and interactive frameworks that reimagine gathering. Brian's work has been featured on Best of the Year lists, has received recognition for Outstanding Direction from *NOW Magazine* and Best Production at SummerWorks 2017, and has been nominated for Outstanding Direction by MyEntertainmentWorld. His recent projects engage in game theory and immersion through audience design. Brian is a sessional instructor within the Theatre Department at X University and has been a guest lecturer at the University of Toronto and Simon Fraser University. He completed a Master of Fine Arts at Simon Fraser University's School for the Contemporary Arts in Theatre Game Design and Interdisciplinary Performance Studies. In his spare time, he likes to visit used bookstores, revisit childhood video games, ride his bicycle, play with his dog Amie, and learn how to draw and play the Armenian duduk. Brian currently lives on the unceded Coast Salish territory of the Squamish, Tsleil-Waututh, and Musqueam Nations. www.brianpostalian.com.

With a passion for learning and creativity, Dr. **Jenelle Rouse** (she/her) leads a dual career as an educator with a doctorate in Applied Linguistics (education) and as a visual body-movement artist. She is a firm believer that having sign language as a base is of utmost importance for every Deaf child. Her published dissertation focuses on accessibility to resources that recognize and promote American Sign Language acquisition of young Deaf children. Dr. Rouse has taken on different roles (e.g., artist, panellist, presenter, ASL translator, co-collaborator, co-researcher, co-writer, and consultant) while working with a variety of academic-, education-, and arts-related projects such as the Ontario College of Teachers, Black Deaf Canada, Sync, Tangled Art + Disability, VibraFusionLab, Canadian Cultural Society of the Deaf, Bodies in Translation, and more. Additionally, she is a founder of Multi-Lens Existence, a project that enables her to continue exploring and experimenting with different mediums to illuminate stories and information, often without any reliance on sound/music.

Jonathan Seinen is an award-winning theatre artist. His most recent directing credits include Ho Ka Kei's *Iphigenia and the Furies (On Taurian Land)*, an adaptation from Euripides commissioned by Saga Collectif and nominated for seven Dora Mavor Moore Awards. Jonathan has worked across the country primarily as a director of new devised collaborative theatre works, with an emphasis on environmental and identity topics and based on field research, autobiography, and the body, working primarily through Architect Theatre (Co-Artistic Producer), lemonTree creations (Artistic Associate 2008–2017), Saga Collectif (Founding Member), and Boys in Chairs Collective (Founding Member). Projects included: Saga Collecif's *Black Boys* and Architect Theatre's *Highway 63: The Fort Mac Show*. Favourite directing credits include *Hamlet* in a community hall, *Deathwatch* by Jean Genet in an art gallery basement, and an undergrad production of *The Visit* by Friedrich Dürrenmatt. He also works as an actor, appearing in new works such as *Body Politic* by Nick Green (lemonTree/Buddies in Bad Times Theatre), *Liberation Days* by David van Belle (Theatre Calgary), and Sean Dixon's *A God In Need Of Help* (Tarragon Theatre). He won the John Hirsch Prize for Directing from the Canada Council for the Arts in 2020, and is a graduate of the University of Alberta, the National Theatre School of Canada, and Columbia University. He is currently Assistant Professor in Theater at SUNY Buffalo State College.

Syrus Marcus Ware is a Vanier scholar, visual artist, community activist, researcher, youth advocate, and educator. For twelve years he was the coordinator of the Art Gallery of Ontario Youth Program. Syrus is currently a facilitator/designer for the Cultural Leaders Lab (Toronto Arts Council and the Banff Centre). He was the inaugural artist-in-residence for the Daniels Spectrum (2016/2017), and is a core member of Black Lives Matter Toronto.

Jessica Watkin is a PH.D. candidate at the University of Toronto's Centre for Drama, Theatre & Performance Studies. Her research is engaged in Disability artists and the way they create performance. She is a Blind multidisciplinary artist, accessibility designer, Disability dramaturge, and educator. She lives in Toronto.